Effective Listening
Key to Your Success

Effective Listening

Key to Your Success

Lyman K. Steil
University of Minnesota and
Communication Development, Inc.

Larry L. Barker
Auburn University and
SPECTRA Communication Associates

Kittie W. Watson
Tulane University and
SPECTRA Communication Associates

McGRAW-HILL PUBLISHING COMPANY
New York St. Louis San Francisco Auckland Bogotá Caracas
Hamburg Lisbon London Madrid Mexico Milan Montreal
New Delhi Oklahoma City Paris San Juan São Paulo Singapore
Sydney Tokyo Toronto

EFFECTIVE LISTENING

Library of Congress Cataloging in Publication Data

Steil, Lyman K.
  Effective listening.

  Includes index.
  1. Communication in management.   2. Listening.
I. Barker, Larry Lee, 1941–   II. Watson, Kittie W.
III. Title.
HD30.3.S75 1983   658.4'52   82-11512
ISBN 0-07-554865-8

First Edition
9876

Preface

This volume is intended to serve as a guide for listening improvement for professionals in business and industry as well as a textbook for use in listening and communication courses in colleges and universities. Each of the authors conducts training seminars in listening for government, business, and industry, education, and the military. This book serves to complement these seminars. Other trainers and organizational communication consultants should find the volume useful in their training seminars, short courses, and workshops. As a textbook, this book has been written with practical applications in mind. Although many reference sources, and studies are alluded to, the text is primarily concerned with building awareness, understanding, and appreciation of listening excellence by the reader. We hope that "students" at all levels will find this book useful toward those ends.

This book owes its origins not only to the combined efforts of the authors, but also to several pioneers in listening research. Dr. Ralph Nichols, the "Father of Listening," of necessity influenced the authors' development and theories of listening. The Sperry Corporation, the "corporate leader in listening enhancement," both directly and indirectly provided an impetus to this volume. Sperry represents *the* corporate model of listening theory applied in the modern organization.

In addition to Dr. Ralph Nichols and the Sperry Corporation, the authors gratefully acknowledge the contributions of many other people who made the final product possible. First, we owe much to friends and colleagues who contributed to Larry Barker's text *Listening Behavior*. Secondly, to

Telstar Productions and Bob Miller, we express sincere appreciation for helping develop the "first" educational video program focusing on listening. Thirdly, to Brian Walker, our thanks for seeing the potential of our project and for helping to get the ball rolling. Fourth, to our many professional colleagues and associates in the International Listening Association, we owe a multinational debt of gratitude. Fifth, we recognize the significant and continuing contributions of our innumerable "clients" in their many "real worlds." Sixth, to a variety of friends, students, and colleagues, our thanks for providing encouragement, examples, and refinement of the manuscript. Finally, but by no means least importantly, our joint appreciation to Dee Steil for her countless contributions to this book.

We hope that you will enjoy the text and profit from its content. If you feel like responding to us by letter or phone concerning the ideas, examples, or illustrations used in the text, please do so—our addresses are listed on page 151.

L.K.S.
L.L.B.
K.W.W.

Contents

Listening Quiz

Before you begin reading this text, answer the following true–false questions regarding the listening process. The answers follow the quiz on the next page.

T ____ F _✓_ 1. Speaking is a more important part of the communication process than listening.

T ____ F _✓_ 2. Since listening requires little energy, it is very easy.

T ____ F _✓_ 3. Listening is an automatic, involuntary reflex.

T ____ F _✓_ 4. Speakers can command listening to occur in an audience.

T _✗_ F _✓_ 5. Hearing ability and listening ability can be used interchangeably.

T _✓_ F ____ 6. When they need to, people can force themselves to listen well.

T ____ F _✓_ 7. The speaker is primarily responsible for the success of communication.

T ____ F _✓_ 8. People listen every day. This daily practice eliminates the need for listening training.

T ____ F _✓_ 9. Competence in listening develops naturally.

T ___ F ___ 10. When you learned to read, you simultaneously learned to listen.

T ___ F ___ 11. Listening is only a matter of understanding the words of the speaker.

T ___ F ___ 12. People remember most of what they hear.

T ___ F ___ 13. Although you may not listen well all the time, when you need to or want to, you can turn your listening ability on and listen well.

T ___ F ___ 14. Your listening cannot be improved.

T ___ F ___ 15. Attitudes are unrelated to listening.

T ___ F ___ 16. Memory and listening are the same thing.

T ___ F ___ 17. You listen as well as you will ever be able to.

T ___ F ___ 18. Listening is primarily impacted by intelligence.

T ___ F ___ 19. Your listening and reading vocabularies are identical.

T ___ F ___ 20. Listening habits cannot be changed.

ANSWERS TO THE LISTENING QUIZ

All of the statements were false. If you marked one or more true, this text should be extremely valuable in helping you gain a deeper understanding about the listening process, and particularly, about the role of active listeners during communication. If you marked all of the statements false, congratulations! You already are aware of some basic principles concerning listening which many people do not recognize. This book should reinforce your ideas regarding listening and help you channel your listening energy more effectively by providing guidelines for isolating listening problems and improving your listening skills.

1
Listening: A 3000 Year Oversight

We have been given two ears and but a single mouth in order that we may hear more and talk less.

Zeno of Citium

Communication has played an essential role in shaping our civilization. Throughout history, communication skills have helped us meet our basic needs in family, work, and social relationships. In everyday life, communication skills allow us to use modern conveniences such as television, radios, or cars, to play poker or bridge, to know if our spouse left dinner in the oven, and to learn how to read this book.

Visualize, if you will, the following communication situations:

(1) You look through an open door of a corporate training seminar where the instructor is delivering his lecture in an extremely entertaining and animated fashion. As you glance around the room, you note that there are no company employees present—just the instructor giving his lecture.

(2) There is an open-air rally at your local courthouse concerning gubernatorial elections. A political candidate is standing on the courthouse steps eloquently outlining his campaign platform to rows and rows of empty chairs.

(3) You walk into a radio station and see one of the latest popular records revolving on a turntable inside the studio. However, as you look around, you find that the station's transmitter is turned off.

It doesn't take a critical observer to note that the basic element missing in each of these situations is an audience or listener. Even with listeners present, there is no assurance that communication is taking place. Communication requires active participation and shared meanings. Communication comes from the Latin word *communis* which means commonness or sharing of meaning. Communication cannot take place without speakers and listeners; even so, many people think of communication as primarily the spoken or written word, and devote little or no time to improving listening skills.

Historically, listening failures have cost lives, time and money. Think about how different life might be if: during the Civil War, the southern army had followed General Lee's order to attack at the Battle of Gettysburg (failure to attack may have altered the course of the war); the captain of the *Titanic* had heeded warnings of approaching icebergs; or Stalin had listened to his intelligence staff's reports regarding Hitler's buildup along the Russian frontier during World War II. These are only a few examples of how poor listening has affected history. Without listening, communication cannot exist; yet, it was not until the early 1900's that listening began to be studied and analyzed independently of speaking.

HOW MUCH TIME DO YOU SPEND COMMUNICATING?

If you stopped to think about how much time you spend communicating, you would probably be surprised. Responding to sounds from alarms, turning on radios, reading morning papers, answering phones, stopping at traffic lights, buying gas from local dealers, getting messages and giving instructions to assistants, writing memos, ordering coffee, and so on—within a few hours you have sent and received thousands of communication messages.

If we communicate this often during a morning, think about the time you spend communicating each day. In 1926, Dr. Paul Rankin first attempted to find out how much time we spend communicating and discovered that adults spend 70% of their waking day in some form of communication. A closer examination of Rankin's study (1929) broke verbal communication into four basic categories.

Type of Communication	Percentage of Time
Writing	9%
Reading	16%
Speaking	30%
Listening	45%

Even in 1926, nearly half of an adult's communication day was spent listening. Other studies conducted since confirm these findings and reveal that, since Rankin's day, mass communication sources such as television and radio have increased the time spent in listening situations (Bird, 1953; Klemmer and Snyder, 1972). For example, in business settings, research indicates that executives spend 63% of their days listening (Keefe, 1971). Moreover, a recent study found that college students spend about 53% of their communication time listening. Another change is that 21% of our listening time is devoted to mass communication sources. The following chart (Barker, et al., 1981) shows other changes:

Type of Communication	Percentage of Time
Writing	14%
Reading	17%
Speaking	16%
Listening	53%
(Other than mass communication, i.e., classrooms, formal, interpersonal)	32%
(Mass communication, i.e., radio, television, music)	21%

As the time spent in different types of communication changes, so does the amount of time we spend communicating. Studies show that, on average, adults now spend 80% of their waking days communicating. If you were to keep a record of your own communication activities during the next 24 hours, how much time do you think you would devote to writing? reading? speaking? listening? Occupational responsibilities have a lot to do with the types of communication you use. Computer programmers spend more time writing and reading, while organizational trainers and developers spend more time speaking. However, if you're typical, over half of your communication time is spent in listening and that percentage increases as people rise in positions of responsibility and authority.

Since so much of your time is devoted to listening, no one can afford the numerous costs associated with even the simplest listening mistakes. Daily activities require you to listen to numerous people in a variety of situations and poor listening can cost you valuable information. We all like to think of ourselves as good listeners; yet how often have you had to reorder supplies, repeat instructions, or explain mistakes caused by listening errors. Off-the-cuff comments such as "He never listens," "I wish someone would teach her to listen," "Why didn't you hear it the first time?" "Didn't you understand?" are common enough.

It is difficult to understand why people do not take listening more seriously when it is so important to job success. However, there seems to be a logical explanation—people have never been trained to listen. That is, there has been a gap in our education. Although we were trained in reading and writing and may have taken courses in speaking, very few of us have received or are receiving training in listening. It is time to close the gaps in our education and learn to listen more effectively. Fortunately, change is now afoot!

LISTENING TRAINING

How did you acquire the ability to listen? Did you take a course in listening techniques? Has your company or organization instituted a listening development program? Probably not. Our listening habits are not the result of training, but rather the result of a lack of training. Listening is a communications skill that we rarely receive formal training in; yet listening is the skill we develop first and use most often. Instead of training, our listening behaviors are developed by watching and listening to others. Infants begin to develop listening behaviors from birth which are observable at 3 to 9 months, speaking skills at 18 to 24 months, and reading and writing skills at 4 to 6 years of age. More importantly, theorists believe that listening and learning go hand in hand (Wood, 1976).

Since we learn listening skills first and use listening skills more than any other communications skill, we might think that there would be formal training in listening during the educational process. Right? *Wrong*! As the "Father of Listening," Dr. Ralph G. Nichols noted in the mid-1950's that "Our schools are upside down." Our educational system spends the most time training students in the skills they use the least (Nichols, 1957). Thirty years later, little has changed. Americans concentrate most on improving our two least used communication skills, writing and reading. Writing and reading are important, of course, but a breakdown of our educational skills training clarifies the challenge (Steil, 1978).

Communication Activities and Training

	Listening	Speaking	Reading	Writing
Learned	1st	2nd	3rd	4th
Used	Most	Next to most	Next to least	Least
	(45%)	(30%)	(16%)	(9%)
Taught	Least	Next to least	Next to most	Most

In a systematic, overt, and directed fashion, our educational system has focused its attention on writing and reading. Approximately 12 years is devoted to writing and 8 years to reading, while little attention is given to speaking and almost none to listening. The relationship between learning and listening is most evident in classroom situations in which as much as 66% of the time is devoted to listening! Professionals who attend special training seminars receive over half their information through listening.

Much of our listening training comes from people who are unaware of their influence. As parents we say, "Listen when I'm speaking to you" or "Don't you know how to listen?" but don't listen when the child talks. Teachers and professionals adapt to poor listener habits by giving key words and phrases such as "This is important to remember," "Pay close attention," "Listen to this" and "Let me repeat." Obviously, indirect methods of learning to listen are not as effective as they could be.

Educators and business executives are concerned with the problems created by ineffective listening. Although, by comparison, there has been little systematic training in listening, we know that listening attitudes and behaviors are learned and since they are learned, they can be improved (Devine, 1967; Steil, 1977; Smeltzer and Watson, 1982). In schools where listening is taught, listening comprehension has as much as doubled in a few months. It is time for us to devote time to listening training.

While improving our listening behavior, there are several points we should keep in mind. First, many adults serve as poor listening models for children. Ineffective role models impact greatly on children's poor listening habits. Second, adult listening behaviors become habitual. Our listening behaviors have been acquired and reinforced over a long period of time. As adults we rarely think about how we listen or consider that it takes time to change old habits. We listen the way we do because we have learned to listen that way. Third, punishing listening behavior tends to produce negative effects which usually causes more serious listening problems. Fourth, people tend to generalize with regard to all types of listening situations and have difficulty in discerning types of listening most appropriate for different situations.

Awareness of these principles should help you understand some of the listening obstacles we face. When listening training is incorporated into our school systems and organizational development programs, we will have more effective communication. Until that time, if we want to be more successful listeners, we need to fill in the gaps in our listening education. This book is designed to fill some of our educational listening gaps by:

(1) explaining the causes, nature, and costs of poor listening;

(2) fostering self-insight into your listening strengths and weaknesses; and

(3) initiating a method of training to improve your listening behavior.

REFERENCES

Barker, L., Edwards, R., Gaines, C., Gladney, K., and Holley, F. An investigation of proportional time spent in various communication activities by college students. *Journal of Applied Communication Research*, **8**, 1980, 101–109.

Bird, D. Teaching listening comprehension. *Journal of Communication.* November 1953, **3**, 127–130.

Devine, T. Listening. *Review of Educational Research*, April 1967, **37**, 152–158.

Keefe, W. F. *Listen Management.* New York: McGraw-Hill, 1971.

Klemmer, E., and Snyder, F., Measurement of time spent communicating. *Journal of Communication*, June 1972, **22**, 142–158.

Nichols, R. and Stevens, L. *Are you Listening?* New York: McGraw-Hill, 1957.

Rankin, P. Listening ability. *Proceedings of the Ohio State Educational Conference's Ninth Annual Session*, 1929.

Smeltzer, L., and Watson, K. W. Improving listening skills used in business: An empirical comparison of discussion length, modeling, and level of incentive. Presented to the International Listening Association Convention, Washington, D.C., 1982.

Steil, L. K. Listen My Students. . . And You Shall Learn. *Towards Better Teaching*, Fall 1978, Vol. 11, No. 12.

Steil, L. K. *A Longitudinal Analysis of Listening Pedagogy in Minnesota Secondary Public Schools.* Unpublished doctoral dissertation, Wayne State University, Detroit, Michigan, 1977.

2
Listening: An Essential Element of Communication

*I know that you believe you understand what
you think I said, but I am not sure you realize
that what you heard is not what I meant.*

Anonymous

All organizational problems have at one time or another
been characterized by a breakdown in communication. Para-
doxically, the panacea or cure-all for these operational
weaknesses has typically been more effective communication.
Concern over potential communication failures has led to a
spate of training seminars and workshops devoted to improving communication skills. In numerous organizations, inhouse training seminars on effective speaking, management
techniques, selling tips, interpersonal effectiveness, or writing
skills have been conducted. While the above skills are essential and should not be minimized, we note that speakers or
sources do not operate independently during communication.
Successful communication also depends on listeners as receivers of messages.

   Concern in recent years about basic communication
skills' effectiveness has led to studies designed to identify the
most important communication needs. In 1978, Dr. Harold
T. Smith undertook a survey of 457 members of the Acade-

my of Certified Administrative Managers who identified "active listening" (hearing how the speaker feels as well as showing concern for the speaker as an individual), as the most critical managerial competency (*Training*, 1978). A similar survey by Professor Jerald Carstens of the University of Wisconsin (River Falls) in 1979 of 45 companies with more than 1000 employees rated listening as the most important communication skill (Mundale, 1980). Even so, of the 45 companies, only nine provided listening skills training for their employees. In 1980, Dr. Aubrey Sanford of the Atlanta Consulting Group undertook a survey of "Fortune 1000" corporation presidents and found poor subordinate listening habits were related to work situations that were most anxiety-producing for top management (Mundale, 1980). The tendency to listen poorly has also been rated as the number-one communication barrier in accountant–accountant relationships and for first-line supervisors (Golen, 1979; Smeltzer, 1979).

Until recently, listeners have been seen as passive participants in communication. Now, however, large numbers of success-oriented people are assuming more active roles and attempting to improve their communications skills by increasing their listening effectiveness. Listening errors are costly and many organizations are now stressing the importance of listening improvement. One corporate leader that has carried the importance of listening to all of its organizational levels is the Sperry Corporation. Paul Lyet, former chief executive of Sperry, says "Effective listening has been an important part of our success, it pays dividends . . ." (Storm, 1980). Listening is so important to Sperry that the company mounted a promotional campaign around the slogan "We understand how important it is to listen." (Courtesy of Sperry Corporation). Central to the success of Sperry's effort was top management's commitment to listening as a corporate philosophy and their revolutionary internal listening training effort. In the initial years of their listening development program, Sperry trained more than 20,000 employees (from top management on down) from more than 30 countries.

The time, money, and talent that Sperry invested resulted in improved employee and customer relations. Similarly, the time and effort you invest in improving your listening skills can work benefits for you. Since all elements of the communication process are important, you need to understand their roles and relationships to become a successful communicator.

COMMUNICATION IN ACTION

Professionals spend nearly 80% of their working days communicating. When communicating you attempt to share a common meaning with another person. Obviously for communication to take place, there must be a sender or source of communication. The sender initiates interactions with a specific purpose in mind. Sources send ideas in the form of verbal (words) or nonverbal (gestures, facial expressions, etc.) *messages*. Each message has unique content (concepts, ideas, words, meaning, etc.) and treatment (delivery, arrangement, etc.). *Channels* of communication carry the messages to their final destination—*listeners* or receivers. Receivers may act upon a message by *sensing* what has been said, *interpreting* what has been heard, *evaluating* what has been sensed and interpreted, and *responding*. When the message is *sensed* in a relatively complete fashion, correctly *interpreted*, and effectively *evaluated*, productive and positive *response* or feedback will hopefully result. Negative or ambiguous feedback will result when the message is not completely sensed, or is misunderstood, or is not effectively evaluated. As feedback is given, the communication process continues over again with the source in the listener or the receiver role. Communication is a dynamic and continuous process that is not, in essence, intermittent. Even "silent treatments" relay messages. No response is a response! In other words, we cannot not communicate!

Communication is influenced by the *context* or situations. You communicate in particular environments, at special times, in unique ways. You make choices about how messages are sent, what channels are used and types of feedback given. Couples avoid arguing in front of friends, company mergers are negotiated behind closed doors, and election results are shared with large crowds of anxious campaign supporters. The quality of communication can be affected at any time. *Noise* or barriers such as telephones ringing, static over radios, babies crying, machinery operating, internal physical or psychological pain cause communication distortion or breakdown.

Among the most influential operating factors during communication are the *filtering agents* of senders and receivers. Similar to filters used with a camera lens, filtering agents allow the passage or blockage or coloring of other elements. Consider how professional photographers use filters designed to let in some rays of light while screening out other rays that may ruin or distort a picture. While a filter is in use, it becomes a part of the camera and affects the final outcome of the picture. Camera filters are changed to get desired results. Similar to a camera lens, filtering agents affect communication with others. Filtering agents such as past work experiences, educational training, opinions, emotions, attitudes, feelings, and language abilities influence how you send and receive messages. Understanding your personal filtering agents puts you in a position to maximize your communication and listening success.

It is critically important for listeners to identify the sender's purpose, because communication breakdowns occur when senders and receivers have different purposes. If you take time off from your busy schedule to attend a paid seminar or a professional conference, you expect to gain information or learn something. If the seminar or conference leader spent the bulk of his or her time on something other than the expected purpose, you would feel frustrated.

The "communication purpose model" shown in Fig. 1.1 identifies *four primary purposes* of human communication. These purposes are contributory to each other and skilled listeners identify and adapt their listening behavior to specific communication purposes. Skilled listeners recognize the im-

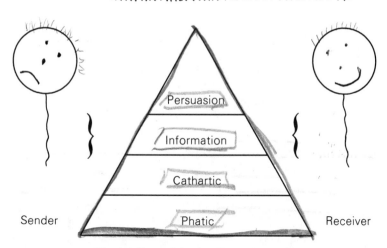

Fig. 1.1 Communication Purpose Model

portance of achieving congruence of purpose. They work hard at correlating sender and receiver purposes. The four communication purposes of *phatic, cathartic, information,* and *persuasion* are primary to professional and personal success.

Phatic ᴇ SMALL talk

Whenever we engage in "small talk," "chit-chat," or conversation that helps us build personal relationships, we are engaging in phatic communication. Many of us may view small talk as unimportant and a waste of time; effective listeners, however, realize it is important and requires a special listening attitude and behavior. Casual chit-chat about the weather, the weekend, the news, the family, the vacation, the World Series, etc., allows a building of personal awareness and a sense of relationship.

Phatic communication helps develop binding relationships and is contributory to all higher-level communication purposes. We may tend to downplay the importance of phatic communication, but in reality, it plays a critical role in our total communication success. As a rule, we generally communicate better at higher levels with people who we're "bound up with" than others with whom we have not developed such relationships. In other words, when our phatic or binding communication diminishes or ceases, our other communication efforts will suffer.

Cathartic   = EMOTIONAL

Catharsis is the process of releasing emotion, the ventilation of feelings, the sharing of problems or frustrations with an empathic listener. Without catharsis, when needed, senders' pent-up emotions and unreleased feelings will result in ulcers, anger, nervous breakdowns, and of course, strained communication. The listener's role is critical since cathartic communication *requires* a caring, empathic, nonjudgmental listener. Catharsis basically requires a *willing* and *able* listener who is observant to the cathartic need cues and clues of others. Individuals in need of catharsis often exude verbal and nonverbal cues, and effective listeners are sensitive to them. Unfortunately numerous individuals purposefully avoid cathartic or unloading communication, since they believe that listening to catharsis takes unwarranted time and energy. In addition, many don't understand the relevance of catharsis, or realize that when it is needed and not allowed, the other purposes of communication will suffer. Cathartic fulfillment is necessary for optimal success at all other levels of communication.

Informational   = INFORM

A third purpose of communication is the sharing of information. The primary goal or purpose of information exchange is the mutual sharing of ideas and data with others. Of course, sharing information with others is one of the most frequent and important purposes of communication. New employees are given informational orientation sessions to learn about company benefits and policies; mechanics listen to automobile owners describe the strange sounds their cars make; students listen to hours of information day in and day out; our dentist shares the value of dental flossing. Politicians, parents, teachers, flight attendants, medical professionals, news and weather forecasters, friends, the clergy and all others engaged in social contact are heavily involved in informational communication, both as senders and receivers. Of course, the ultimate success of informational connection centers on whether or not specific data (information) has been thoroughly transmitted and received, correctly interpreted, effectively evaluated, and responded to. But remember, no one is assured of perfect understanding, accuracy, and response. Consider the following information exchange*:

> A new employee approached one of the women in our office with an important-looking paper in his hand, pointed to the paper-shredding machine and asked her to show him how to operate it. "Of course," she said. "You just turn the switch on here, put your sheet of paper in here, like this, and that's all there is to it."

> As the machine devoured his document, the new man thanked her for her help and then asked, "By the way, how many copies will this make?"

Persuasive Communication

Door-to-door salespeople, antique auctioneers, car dealers, TV and radio pitchmen, or political candidates are the first people who come to mind when thinking about persuasive communication. Other persuasive appeals such as ball point pen advertisements, complimentary matches from your favorite restaurant, family portraits on office desks, or wearing three-piece suits go relatively unnoticed as forms of persuasion. Persuasive communication attempts to (1) reinforce existing attitudes and beliefs, (2) instil new attitudes and beliefs, or (3) affect behaviors and actions. All communication is essentially persuasive in that we want our ideas to be ac-

---

*Gary Seering and Durreshahwar Baig, *Reader's Digest*, June, 1980, p. 184. Reprinted by permission.

cepted and liked. However, the success of persuasive communication depends on a person's conscious or unconscious listening. Many commercials appeal to unconscious buyers who are unaware that persuasion took place even when they enter checkout lines with products in hand.

Communication purposes rarely operate independently of each other and are often difficult to isolate. Nevertheless, senders as well as receivers of messages usually have, at a given moment, a primary purpose or goal of communication. A civic group may think a speaker has come to discuss the dangers of inflation when actually his primary purpose may be to sell silver coins as investments. We tend to seek out situations and interactions that are consistent with our own purposes. Difficulties arise when speakers' and listeners' stated purposes and intended purposes do not coincide.

CONGRUENCE OF PURPOSE

Effective and productive listeners distinguish among the different communication purposes, since each purpose calls for a different listening approach. Phatic communication requires time, patience, an other-orientedness, and a recognition of the larger value of relationship building. Cathartic communication requires caring, concerned, risk-taking and nonjudgmental listening. Truly empathic people suspend evaluation and criticism when they listen to others. Here the challenge is to enter into the private world of the speaker, to understand without judging actions or feelings. By contrast, the task of listening to a persuasive speaker eventually involves evaluating the speaker's case and deciding whether we agree or disagree, and then taking appropriate action.

Significant failures in listening result when the speaker and listener communicate at cross-purposes. We've all experienced individuals who attempt to persuade us before providing the necessary information needed to make a rational decision. By the same token, people who engage in catharsis when we desire hard data about a problem do not communicate well. As good listeners, we must consciously ask ourselves four questions: What is the speaker's purpose? What is my purpose for listening? How can I act to align those purposes? What special listening requirements does any given purpose call for?

It's important to note that, as Fig. 1.1 suggests, these four purposes are hierarchical in nature. Phatic communication provides the basis for the other three purposes of communication, often coming before and laying the ground work for catharsis, information, and persuasion. Similarly, a person desperately needing catharsis will not be able to effectively transmit information or persuade others until his or her emotional needs have been met. Finally, we know that persuasive communication must be based upon evidence and information before it can be truly successful.

LEVELS OF COMMUNICATION

One advantage of talking to yourself is that you know at least somebody's listening.

Franklin P. Jones

Communication is often thought of as simply a matter of sending messages between two people; however, we participate in communication on several levels daily. Communication that takes place inside you is intrapersonal communication. You constantly communicate with yourself by planning the day's agenda, controlling your temper, or making decisions to get out of bed. Even in intrapersonal communication, we communicate at any given moment for a specific communication purpose. Socrates once said, "Know thyself." It is important for us to learn to listen to ourselves. As we communicate well with ourselves at the intrapersonal level, we will more likely communicate well with others at the interpersonal and public levels.

Job interviews, telephone conversations, marital and family interactions and business meetings are examples of interpersonal communication or person-to-person communication. Listening is essential since each person plays the role of speaker and listener simultaneously. Group communication occurs when three or more people get together. Successful group encounters provide all members with the opportunity to participate. Of course, active participation includes listening as part of the communication process.

Public communication, or one person addressing a group, usually places the primary focus for communication success on the speaker; however, without an audience composed of effective listeners, no productive communication would exist. Mass communication such as TV and radio is characterized by mechanical reproduction, rapid distribution, and delayed feedback. Listeners can usually cope with more distractions when tuned to mass communication. Receivers or listeners may, for instance, leave televisions on while talking on the phone, answering questions from others, or reading a newspaper.

Although the occasions, environments, situations, and participant relationships are different in the foregoing examples, and have an impact on the listening task, it is also obvious that there are numerous common listening elements in all contexts.

Organizations typically exhibit all levels of communication. Learning to listen well at lower communication levels (for example, phatic vs. persuasion) makes listening easier at other levels when necessary. As you begin to identify some of your filtering agents, types of interactions, potential distractions and communication strengths you will be in a better position to control your communication effectiveness.

WHO HAS THE PRIMARY RESPONSIBILITY FOR COMMUNICATION?

Earlier we mentioned that communication responsibility has been historically placed on the speaker in this society. Should this necessarily be so? Senders and receivers both have the ability to control elements during the communication process, so who should accept primary responsibility for communication success, the speaker or the listener? In other words, if communication breakdowns occur, who is to blame? Of the thousands of people throughout the United States, who have been asked this question during our seminars, 70% believe the primary responsibility for communication success rests with the speaker, 25% with the listener, and 5% fail to respond. Those who believe that speakers hold the primary responsibility contend that:

1. Senders initially control the communication act.

2. Senders hold a vested interest in communication.

3. Senders determine the primary and secondary purposes of the specific communication.

4. Senders analyze filtering agents of receivers and develop messages for specific audiences.

5. Senders select the channels for communication.

6. Senders choose the context for communication.

7. Senders observe and receive feedback from which to evaluate.

Those that view receivers as primarily responsible have similar arguments, such as:

1. Receivers have the power to accept or reject the communication.

2. Receivers determine the meaning of the communication.

3. Receivers control the channel of the communication.

4. Receivers control the feedback factors of communication.

5. Receivers control the context of the communication.

Both sides have valid arguments, but either view places speakers and listeners in passive positions. Individuals agreeing with the 70% who give primary responsibility to speakers, in a sense say that listeners should participate from the standpoint of: "Ok, I'm here . . . now you'd better . . . make it interesting, keep my attention, have something valuable to say, and . . . ." Similarly, 25% of the general public give listeners the primary responsibility, by their response, for making sure that messages are ethical, well researched, organized and interesting. In either case, these viewpoints have one interesting characteristic in common: shifting the burden for success to others and thus letting others control their behavior or destinies. In work, home, social, church, and educational situations, there are millions of us who place the primary burden of communication success on others. Yet, who is in the best position to control your own future? You are of course and because you are, *you* need to be the more responsible co-municator.

As skilled listeners, we need to take a position different from others. Our challenge is to accept a "minimum 51% responsibility" for communication success no matter if we are in the role of sender or receiver. Your mission—"if you decide to accept it"—will positively affect your communication and listening behavior. In every communication situation, regardless of purpose, you play primary roles of senders and receivers of messages. Picture yourself as wearing two hats: one hat is your sender hat and one hat is your receiver hat. During communication, you constantly change these hats. Now imagine a third hat: a minimum 51% responsibility hat. See yourself as wearing it at all times. When used as the foundation for the other hats, this third hat will make you a more successful communicator. Using all three hats, regardless of your momentary role during communication, will move you from passive through responsible to active communication. Your acceptance, constant practice, and real commitment will aid you *both* as a sender and as a receiver. But due to our typical existing beliefs and consequent practices, this acceptance of the minimum 51% responsibility will serve you most as listener. Try it, you"ll buy it!

THE SIER MODEL: THE FOUR STAGES OF LISTENING

The listening act really consists of four connected activities—sensing, interpreting, evaluating and responding. Taking the first letter from each of these terms, we arrive at the S–I–E–R Model represented in Fig. 2.1.

Listening is not synonymous with hearing, but good listening begins at the level of sensing the sender's message. Sensing is basic to the other three activities involved in listening—if the listener does not sense the message, he or she can do nothing further with it.

After the message is sensed, a second activity comes into play: accurate interpretation. Here we encounter semantic problems: the sensitive listener asks, "I heard the words used by the speaker, but am I assigning a comparable meaning to them?" Effective listeners remember that "words have no meaning—people have meaning." The assignment of meaning to a term is an internal process; meaning comes from inside us. And although our experiences, knowledge, and attitudes differ, we often misinterpret each other's messages while under the illusion that a common understanding has been achieved.

Active listeners go beyond sensing and interpretation to another act: evaluation. Here the listener decides whether or

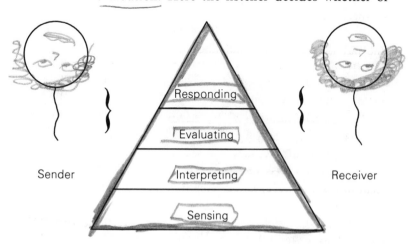

Fig. 2.1 SIER: Communication Stages Model

not to agree with the speaker. The evidence is weighed, fact is sorted from opinion, and judgment is rendered. Poor listeners begin this activity too soon, often hearing something they disagree with and tuning out the speaker from that point on. When this occurs, sensing and interpretation stop —so does listening. Speakers have the right to be heard, and the best listeners delay judgment until the message is fully presented. Moreover, the best listeners work hard at developing their judgmental skills and abilities.

Finally, to be complete, the listening process must result in response. Responses can be of many kinds, ranging from nonverbal cues to the speaker showing that we've received the message (smiling, frowning), to giving the speaker feedback, asking questions, and requesting clarification. Ultimately the listener asks, "What's expected of me now? What action, if any, should result?"

Every effective executive realizes the critical importance of responding. Ultimately, the ability to respond is linked to a sense of responsibility. The meaning of responsibility when applied to listening was well expressed by Erich Fromm in *The Art of Loving*: "Today responsibility is often meant to denote duty, something imposed on one from the outside. But responsibility, in its true sense, is an entirely voluntary act. . . . To be responsible means to be ready and able to 'respond.'"

The response stage of listening is especially crucial for judging the success of the listening act as a whole. This is true because the first three stages—sensing, interpreting, and evaluating—are internal acts. They take place inside of us; no one can directly observe them. Until the listener makes a concrete response, it's often difficult to determine whether the speaker has been successful in getting the point across. The response stage (see Fig. 2.1) is the first to include behaviors we can see and measure. If there is a breakdown at any stage (S, I, E, or R), it will not be apparent until the response stage.

These four stages of listening are hierarchical, just as the purposes of communication. The message must be sensed before it can be interpreted or evaluated. And one cannot intelligently respond to a message until it's been properly evaluated, interpreted and sensed. Any failure at the sensing level will impede success at the "higher" levels. And the listener who evaluates a message before correctly understanding it does not understand the complete nature of the listening process.

When faced with communication breakdowns, we usually wonder what went wrong. The SIER model can be used as a *diagnostic* tool to determine at what level the observed communication breakdown started. Although we always see the *response* level results, the first point to remember when diagnosing a listening breakdown is to look for the lowest level where the breakdown could have started. In ascending order from S to I, I to E, and E to R, we need to check all levels of the listening process to determine the point of origin.

Of course when diagnosing a problem, there is no way to be absolutely certain about the level of error since we cannot see inside another person's head. However, by looking at external signs and indications we can make a good guess as to where the problem started. Again, we have to look to the lowest level at which the problem could have started. Otherwise, we may be diagnosing a symptom rather than a cause of the actual communication problem. See if you can identify the lowest-level errors in the following situations.

In 1938 Hitler's invasion of Czechoslovakia caused tension in the United States. On October 30, 1938, millions of Americans tuned their radios to CBS's "Mercury Theatre of the Air" to be entertained. That night Orson Welles introduced H. G. Well's *War of the Worlds* and attempted to control possible side effects by broadcasting repeated warnings that the radio play newscast was fictional and not to be taken seriously. However, the program set off a nation-wide panic with audiences believing aliens from Mars had invaded New Jersey. Thousands of calls were made to the news media, many people reported seeing aliens, there were huge traffic jams, and U.S. troops were alerted for action. Because of its impact, FCC passed regulations prohibiting future fictional news bulletins.

At first, this example might seem to be focused at the response level, but we have to look for the origin of the problem. For many, this situation was probably caused by a sensing error and we know that sensing problems cause errors with interpretation, evaluation and response. Many people who panicked did not sense the repeated warnings of a fictitious broadcast. Thus their ultimate processing and response was inappropriate. In this case, when segments of a message were missed, important information was lost.

As listeners, we need to think about ways to improve our ability to sense a message accurately. It may help to select a better place to sit, turn up the volume on the radio or television, eliminate overriding distractions, controlling emotions, taking notes, or asking for repetition. Repeating a message several times is often a useful device to help people hear a message, but as with the *War of the Worlds* broadcast, repeated warnings were not effective either. Our mind-set often causes us to hear what we expect to hear. Now let's look at a second illustration.

> Saturday, March 1, 1980, was the first time the U. S. had supported a United Nations Security Council resolution sharply criticizing Israel. Two days later on March 3, 1980, the White House reported that a mistake had been made in their Security Council vote. According to *Time Magazine* here is what happened.
>
> On February 28th, 14 members of the Security Council approved a draft of a resolution condemning settlement of the Arab populated West Bank by Israelis. A copy of the proposal was sent by U. S. Ambassador McHenry to Secretary of State Vance in hopes of presidential approval. The President had three reservations. Vance was directed to tell McHenry to abstain unless (1) the council deleted a paragraph implying that Israel did not guarantee religious freedom, (2) McHenry had reservations about the wording of a controversial paragraph demanding dismantling of all Israeli settlements, and (3) all references to Jerusalem were excised from the text.
>
> Confusion surrounded Carter's third reservation. According to Vance's aide, he thought Carter was concerned only about

the mentioning of Jerusalem in the controversial paragraph. Vance did not tell McHenry that every reference to Jerusalem had to be removed. McHenry met the President's requirements according to Vance. Vance telephoned the President on Saturday morning before the vote and Vance told Carter that the references to Jerusalem were removed, although Vance knew that was not literally true. The President did not ask for Vance to read the final proposal and gave his approval to vote yes.

Basically, Carter and Vance had an interpretation problem. Vance was instructed to remove *all* references to Jerusalem, but Vance did not take the president literally. If Carter had asked for the proposal to be read or had had a copy to read himself, maybe the United States would have avoided worldwide scorn and ridicule. You have probably experienced a situation in which messages were interpreted differently than you had intended, and have an understanding how easily interpretation errors occur. The next example is the result of a different type of listening error.

In 1972, Richard Grimshaw, 13, was riding with a neighbor on a road near San Bernardino, California when another automobile plowed into the rear of their car. Their gas tank ruptured and 90% of Richard's body was badly burned. Today, Richard is still receiving operations to help repair his body.

In court, the plaintiffs charged that the manufacturer's crash testing research had revealed weaknesses in their gas tanks which caused excessive gas leakage upon impact. However, the company chose not to spend the ten dollars per car it would have taken to correct the weaknesses. The result was a $128.5 million jury verdict in favor of the plaintiff.

In this situation, evidently someone had heard and interpreted the message correctly, but the appropriate response was not taken. So where did the problem occur? It appears that someone made a judgment that the gas leakage and weak tanks were not serious problems. However, this evaluation resulted in consequences that caused suffering for everyone concerned. This example could just as easily have been a success story if the message had been evaluated differently. Incorrect judgments ultimately create reaction or response problems and the potential for communication breakdowns.

Let's look at one last seemingly small example, although we know the resulting problems add to significant consequences.

A company softball team ordered uniforms for all of its players. The captain of the team went to a local sporting goods store and ordered 18 uniforms. Each uniform was to have the player's name embroidered above the front shirt pocket and the company name Union Carboneers sewn on the back of the shirt in large letters visible to spectators. The salesperson took the order and repeated the information and agreed that the company name would be a good advertising device. Two weeks later when the uniforms arrived the uniforms had the company name above the front pocket and the players' names in large letters on the back of the shirts. The captain refused the shipment.

What happened? We know the salesperson heard the instructions, since he repeated exactly what was expected. It's possible that the salesperson did not understand the order. On the other hand, it may be that the salesperson made a poor judgment and did not think that the lettering mattered. Then what went wrong? It seems that the problem started at the response level. Somehow the sporting goods store responded differently than what they intended and lost money and future business. Perhaps the salesperson heard, understood, agreed, but simply forgot. We know he didn't respond appropriately. There have probably been situations in which you have responded differently than you had planned. When situations like this occur, it is not a sensing, interpreting, or evaluation problem; it is a response problem.

These few examples show that communication can be successful at one level and still fail at higher levels. By using the SIER model to diagnose problems that have occurred, applying communication principles to correct the problem, and planning ways to prevent communication breakdowns, you can improve your listening and communication effectiveness.

Communication is more complex than listening to an occasional message. Secretaries remind managers of appointments while they talk on the telephone, sign letters, and listen to employee complaints. Professionals are often bombarded by several messages and reach points of information overload. Communication situations change so quickly that many difficulties go undetected until days or weeks after the fact. Some time ago, for example, President Carter told his aides to call the military commander at Fort Chaffee, Arkansas. The order instructed the commander to use the force necessary to restrain Cuban refugees. That order never reached the commander and consequently on June 3, 1980, the Army backed down when Cubans awaiting relocation started running for the gates. The riot that ensued left 60 people injured and four buildings burned to the ground. Although Carter had issued an order, no one knew there was a breakdown in communication until it was too late.

EXPANDED SIER MODEL

As we have considered the SIER model to this point, we have viewed the communication and listening process primarily with respect to a "frozen frame moment." To reflect the dynamics of the real world, the "expanded SIER model" (Fig. 3.1) clarifies the overlap of levels in the ongoing communication process. This sawtooth model illustrates the ascending-order requirement associated with the challenge of fulfilling your commitment as a listener.

Each person who takes part in the communication process brings unique filtering agents to the interaction. The expanded SIER model shows how our interactions progress through time. As we switch back and forth between sender and receiver roles, we sense, interpret, evaluate, and respond

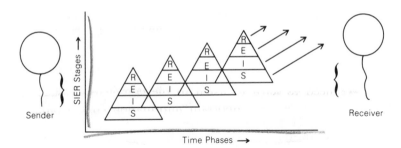

Fig. 3.1 SIER Sawtooth Process Model

simultaneously. If a communication breakdown occurs, we usually think of one error as causing the problem. However, through the model, you can see that the potential for errors during communication is limitless. This model represents the interaction between two people, but think about the increased complexity as you add other people to the conversation.

As more people are added to conversations, the potential for misunderstandings multiplies. Errors occur at different communication levels, with senders and receivers, and at the beginning, middle, and end of interactions. Errors in initial meetings usually cause breakdowns in later meetings. We can all think of times we've failed to listen to an entire message because we felt that we already knew what a person was going to say. At times our expectations are accurate, but sometimes they are not. An example from *Reader's Digest** highlights this point.

> When their son left for his freshman year at Duke University, his parents gave him a Bible, assuring him it would be a great help. Later, as he began sending them letters asking for money, they would write back telling him to read his Bible, citing chapter and verse. He would reply that he was reading the Bible—but he still needed money.

---

*Contributed by John T. Spach *Reader's Digest*, March 1980, p. 197. Reprinted by permission.

When he came home for a semester break, his parents told him they knew he had not been reading his Bible. How? They had tucked $10 and $20 bills by the verses they had cited in their letters.

We need to learn to listen to the complete message so we won't miss out on important information later. Communicating with different purposes or errors is likely to cause serious communication failures. Whenever there are difficulties initially, think of a possibility of future misunderstanding.

A president of a large southern power company mentioned that his greatest frustration takes place with retiring employees. He has learned not to mention the possibility of work after retirement or even how much a person will be needed because he's often misinterpreted. Once he mentioned the possibility of future consulting with a retiring employee and later found the employee telling other employees that the company was making a policy exception in his case so that he could work past the age of 65. When the president confronted him again and repeated that he could not work past 65, the employee got angry and believed the president had gone back on his word.

Obviously, the president and employee had different communication purposes as well as at least one level of listening error. Avoiding the issue is not the best solution. In the example above, the president assumed that a listening error occurred. This is probably the case, since the employee seemed only to listen to what he wanted to hear. However, the president could also look at his own communication to see if there were any errors on his part. At the time of the first interaction, he could have asked the employee to repeat what he said to make sure that there were no sensing errors. Then he could have asked the employee to explain what he had said to check for interpretation errors. Again looking at the lowest level of interaction helps us to detect more than just a symptom in a communication breakdown.

TYPES OF LISTENING

We mentioned earlier that many people have difficulty in adapting their level of listening to different situations. Most of us participate in two types of listening contexts: social and serious (Barker, 1971). We listen informally in social situations such as coffee breaks, concerts, or dinner table talk. We take part in serious listening in formal situations such as contract negotiations, loan requests, and jury duty.

Four types of social listening that may be associated with conversation or entertainment are: appreciative listening, conversational listening, courteous listening, and listening to indicate love or respect.

Appreciative listening involves recognizing aspects of a speaker's style, interpreting characters in a dialogue, listening for rhythm in music, or visualizing images from hearing a message. When we listen to a poem being read, a concert, a play, or a TV program, we listen appreciatively. With appreciative listening comes some sort of satisfaction or pleasure from active participation.

Conversational listening involves two-way communication. Conversational listening may also take place in serious situations, but generally, it is seen as social listening because of the informal settings in which it occurs. If you think about the conversations you've had in a typical day, you'll find that the best conversationalists are also good listeners. Courteous listening includes conversation, but you are primarily involved as a listener. This is sometimes a difficult role to play because we usually enjoy talking. We use courteous listening when listening to employees complain about paperwork or try out their ideas for a new safety training program.

A type of listening that goes along with courteous listening is listening to indicate love or respect. Unfortunately, we often neglect the importance of listening with love and respect. When a parent listens to a child say something which may not be important to the parent but is extremely important to the child, or when a child listens to an elderly parent tell the same stories over and over again, he or she listens with love and respect.

Serious listening can be classified as either selective or concentrated listening. Selective listening involves listening only to segments of a message. Concentrated listening involves listening to the entire message and attempting to take in all aspects of what is said. At times we need to remember everything that has been said, while other times all the information may not need to be remembered. Unfortunately, some listeners do not realize that they are listening selectively. Selective listening may result from poor listening habits and if you find yourself missing important information, then maybe you have been using selective listening inappropriately.

Serious listening is divided into subcategories of critical and discriminative listening. Critical listening attempts to analyze information offered as evidence, and make critical judgments about the validity and quality of materials presented. We analyze politician platforms, architects' plans, and the ideas in advertising campaigns. Discriminative listening is intended for understanding and remembering. When you try to remember directions from a service station attendant in a new city, relay a message to a client, or listen to a question asked of you during a press interview, you take place in discriminative listening.

Although it is important to be aware of the types of listening, a situation can rarely be characterized by only one type of listening. For example, after you talk about your birdie putt, you might talk about the latest Supreme Court decision concerning tax deductions. Like communication itself, listening is a process and we need to keep in mind that in one situation we engage in a variety of types of listening.

NONVERBAL LISTENING

He that has eyes to see and ears to hear may convince himself that no mortal can keep a secret. If his lips are silent, he chatters with his finger tips; betrayal oozes out of him at every pore.

Freud

One important type of listening that does not require the ability to hear is nonverbal listening. The deaf "listen"—often very well—through alternative channels of sight, taste, smell, and touch. Those of us who can hear are at a distinct advantage over deaf listeners, yet we often fail to capitalize on our advantage.

Many of our daily decisions are based on information derived through channels other than hearing, although we rarely stop to think about the importance of total sensory listening. Think for a moment about what it would be like to communicate only through sounds. Without all our senses, many of the communication experiences such as tastes of food, a lover's embrace, spectator sports, and familiar smells would be lost. Of the senses we take for granted, one of the most valuable besides hearing is sight.

Recently there has been increased interest in nonverbal aspects of communication. Body language, facial expression, eye contact, vocal characteristics, clothing, and spatial distances often substitute for verbal forms of communication. We all know that information comes from what a person *does* as well as what a person *says*, and we run the risk of misinterpreting information when we fail to consider both. Think about the importance of nonverbal behavior. Dressing for employment interviews, employees who arrive late for work, pats on the back from company presidents, shutting doors to inner offices, and avoiding angry clients all communicate messages nonverbally. In fact, when verbal and nonverbal messages contradict each other, we have a tendency to believe the nonverbal message (Mehrabian, 1972). Glancing at your watch, putting on your jacket, and looking at the door often signal that you need or want to leave even when verbally you may say "Sure, I have time to look over your new proposal."

We cannot avoid communicating, the clothes we wear, the way we sit, the arrangement of our offices, and even the cars we drive communicates information to ourselves and others. It is important to gain greater awareness of how we communicate nonverbally in order to reduce chances for sensing, interpreting, evaluating, and responding erroneously. Combined sensitivity concerning verbal and nonverbal messages will increase your probability of listening success in everyday relationships.

SUMMARY

By now you should have a clearer understanding of elements in the communication process. The complexity of communication lies in the dual role played by listeners and senders of messages. Accepting the minimum 51% responsibility both as sender or receiver in all communication situations increases our chances for successful listening. Phatic, cathartic, informational, persuasive, and entertainment communication are stages of communication that apply to our communication relationships whether on the level of intrapersonal, interpersonal, groups, organization, public or mass.

Because of the complexity of communication, we often have breakdowns. The SIER formula helps us detect the lowest level in which errors occur. Analysis of sensing, interpreting, evaluating, and responding levels helps both senders and receivers detect communication breakdowns. The SIER model locates difficulties in social and serious listening situations when verbal communication breakdowns occur. We should also be aware of the role of nonverbal communication because nonverbal messages may relay as much information as verbal messages. Up to this point we have emphasized the complexity of communication and the importance of listening in the communication process. In the next chapter we will consider ways to help you identify your listening strengths and weaknesses.

REFERENCES

Barker, L. *Listening Behavior.* Englewood Cliffs, NJ: Prentice-Hall, 1971.

Conigliaro, S. Listen your way to the top. *Graduating Engineer,* Winter 1980, 15–17.

Golen, S. An analysis of communication barriers in public accounting firms. *The Journal of Business Communication,* **17**, 1980, 39–49.

Mehrabian, A. *Nonverbal Communication.* Chicago: Aldine-Atherton, 1972.

Mundale, S. Why more CEO's are mandating listening and writing training. *Training,* October 1980, 37–41.

Smeltzer, L. Barriers to effective communication for the first line supervisor: Implications for the instructor of business communication. *Proceedings* American Business Communication National Convention, 1979, 173–178.

Storm, B. Sperry Corporation. *Madison Avenue,* February 1980, **22**, 50, 54.

The 20% activities that bring 80% payoff. *Training,* June 1978, 6.

3

Are You Getting the Most From Your Listening?

As friends, we don't see eye to eye, but then we don't hear ear to ear either.

Buster Keaton

You hear thousands of messages each day. Listening is central to your professional and personal success. But skilled listening is more than just sensing what has been said; you also have to interpret, evaluate and respond to what is said. Listening is a major communication activity, yet 80% of people surveyed rated their listening ability as average or lower (Steil, 1980). Clearly that's not good enough for successful communication. As we have seen, many businesses have not established training programs to improve employee listening habits and poor listeners are apt to make more mistakes which translate into lost revenues. Marriage counselors claim that a major cause of divorce is poor communication. For this reason, before saying "I do" many churches require couples to attend communication training sessions that stress the importance of listening in relationships.

WHY LEARN?

The greatest problem in communication is the illusion that it has been accomplished.

Daniel W. Davenport

In its landmark campaign to improve listening skills of its employees, Sperry Corporation came up with an advertisement headlined:

KNOWING HOW TO LISTEN
COULD DOUBLE THE EFFICIENCY
OF AMERICAN BUSINESS.
DID YOU HEAR THAT?
(*Courtesy of Sperry Corporation*)

The point was made:

Business today is held together by its communication system.

And listening is undoubtedly its weakest link.

Most of us spend about half our business hours listening. Listening poorly. Research studies show that on the average we listen at a 25% level of efficiency.

A statistic that is not only suprisingly low, but terribly costly.

With more than 100 million workers in America, a simple ten dollar listening mistake by each of them would cost a billion dollars.

Letters have to be retyped; appointments rescheduled; shipments reshipped.

And when people in large corporations fail to listen to one another, the results are even costlier.

Unfortunately, many mistakes cost much, much more. When people fail to listen, the results can be devastating.

A large engineering firm had a team of 24 engineers working on a major military project at a cost of about $1000 per man per week, plus an independent engineering consultant whose fee was $4,000 per week. The team encountered a critical problem that threatened to delay the entire project and subject the firm to a heavy penalty for lateness under its contract. So the head of the project telephoned the consultant, assigned him to work out a solution to the problem, and specified that the company must absolutely have the solution in one week. Later the project head told one of our authors, "At the end of the week, I again telephoned the engineer and learned he had been working on an entirely different phase of the problem than the one for which we needed a solution. Obviously, I had failed to make clear to him what we needed. But in our original conversation, he had indicated that he understood what needed to be done. So I had to divert all our engineers on the project until we got the solution."

The cost of this breakdown:

The consultant's fee for one week	$4,000
Salaries and fringe benefits of company engineers	24,000
Penalty for lateness under the company's contract	122,000
Total:	$150,000

(Steil, 1979)

Ideas get distorted by as much as 80% as they travel through the chain of command. Even those distortions that do not cost money can affect employee relations. Employees feel more and more distant, and ultimately alienated from top management. Alienation hurts organizational morale and productivity. Employees need to feel that someone is listening.

Listening is critical to your success, and most listening skills are learned by chance. A recent survey of executives in 72 major corporations emphasizes that good listening skills don't come naturally (*Corporate Report*, 1979). Our hit-or-miss educational system is not working. Research shows that most of us are partially effective as listeners and need improvement. Much of what is heard is not remembered. Over

30 years of research clearly indicates that we listen at approximately 25% effectiveness and efficiency (Dietze and Jones, 1931, Steil, 1975). In other words, on average, we deal productively with about ¼ of what we listen to! Is that good enough? A buyer in a large retail clothing chain did not think so—especially after she received 800 pairs of a line of fall shoes after placing a phone order for 80. There are simply too many people who do not listen as well as they should or could.

Think for a moment about communication breakdowns you have experienced at work, at home, or socially. What resulted from the confusion? Did the misunderstanding cause the loss of an important business account, a divorce, arrival at a party on the wrong night, or failure on a driving examination? The most serious communication breakdowns are usually caused by poor listening. Listening mistakes cost time, money, human relationships, psychological and physical pain, lawsuits, and more.

Costs of Poor Listening

With the demands of modern living, we value our time. It would be difficult for most of us to place a price tag on the value of a few hours alone with someone special, the latest best-selling novel, or sailing on a lake. Our time is precious, yet we frequently lose time through ineffective communication and listening errors. You make plans for a dinner date tonight; your guests planned to come tomorrow. You thought your partner said Columbus, Ohio, not Columbus, Georgia. Recently, while waiting at an airport a businessman was overheard telling his wife, "Honey, I CAN'T HELP IT! The secretary must have told me the wrong day. I'll fly home later tonight and come back next week! There's no use arguing about it now."

Lost time is an inconvenience and often places strains on relationships. People often get too busy to listen and relationships dissolve with notes saying "I need someone to listen, and he (she) does . . ." Children are crushed when parents forget little league games, birthday parties or family outings. You may hear what someone is telling you without really listening to the meaning.

Communication errors not only cost disrupted relationships; they also cause physical and psychological pain. Occasionally we hear reports of hospital patients receiving the wrong operation. One New Orleans patient (Mr. Johnston) reported that orderlies came in and told him it was time for his operation. Mr. Johnston was a little surprised since he checked in only two hours earlier. The orderlies assured him that the doctor requested him to be brought to the operating room. In the elevator, Mr. Johnston asked if knee operations were always conducted so quickly. The orderlies looked at each other and said "You're having an abdominal operation!" Sensing that Mr. Johnston was nervous about his operation, they failed to listen to his explanation. Eventually the doctor was called and the orderlies went to get another Mr. Johnston who was on the same floor.

Historically, poor listening has led to devastating consequences, as the following descriptions of military and aviation disasters indicate.

In 1940 Americans deciphered a Japanese secret code referred to as MAGIC. Breaking the code enabled the United States to detect Japanese war maneuvers. Throughout 1941 Washington issued warnings to military commanders in Hawaii to be prepared for war with Japan. Even though these warnings confirmed the commanders' expectations, they didn't think that Pearl Harbor was threatened. The commanders increased air reconnaissance in the Pacific, but not north of Hawaii. On November 27, 1941 a stronger warning was issued stating that aggressive action was expected from Japan in the next few days. Again, the commanders believed that the target could not be their own base.

On December 7, 1941, the Japanese destroyed the United States Pacific Fleet at Pearl Harbor. When Japanese planes arrived over Pearl Harbor, no alert was sounded until the Japanese bombs began to explode. The attack began at 8:00 on Sunday morning, when most of the naval officers and enlisted men were on leave or just getting up from their bunks. The Japanese bombed 96 anchored American ships. They sank or damaged all eight battleships, three cruisers, and four other vessels in the harbor. Over 2,000 men were killed and at least 2,000 more were listed as wounded or missing. Most of the Navy and Army buildings and aircraft installations were completely destroyed and many considered Pearl Harbor the worst military disaster in American history.

The military authorities at Pearl Harbor had been warned, yet not one really listened. Some probably didn't sense the warnings; some probably didn't correctly interpret them; some probably didn't effectively evaluate them and of course the response was not adequate.

In the worst aviation disaster in history, to date, we see communication and listening failure at the heart of tragedy.

On March 27, 1977, a KLM 747 with 248 passengers and a Pan American 747 with 380 vacationers prepared to take off from the fog-shrouded airport at Tenerife in the Canary Islands. The KLM pilot was directed by the control tower to taxi up the runway, make a 180 degree turn and "Standby for take-off clearance." Meanwhile the Pan American 747 was directed by the same control tower to taxi up the same foggy runway and turn off at the third off ramp. There were four exits from the runway to the taxi way. The Pan American crew, however, considered the first turn to be inactive because it was blocked by other aircraft. So the Pan Am crew headed for the fourth instead of third exit. Nevertheless, the tower made a request and Pan Am acknowledged that they would report when clear of the runway.

Both planes and the control tower were tuned to the same radio frequency and should have heard the various communication exchanges between all parties. Yet, according to a nine minute tape recording, no clearance was given to the KLM 747 to take off. Evidently, the KLM pilot misunderstood his instructions. The KLM 747 attempted to take off and when the pilot saw the other 747, he was approaching at 186 miles per hour and there was no way to avoid a collision that cost:

581 lives
$500 million in lawsuits (many still are in court)
2 Boeing 747's worth $63 million dollars

If both pilots and the control tower had fully sensed, properly interpreted and evaluated, and responded appropriately, the worst disaster in aviation history might have been avoided. Extreme examples like these emphasize the costs of poor listening and the need for improving listening effectiveness.

Rewards of Effective Listening

Like any other skill, listening requires active commitment and effort. As mentioned earlier, active participation is necessary in serious and social situations. Serious listening during contract negotiations, loan requests, political speeches, training seminars, or jury duty requires one or more of the following abilities: comprehension, retention, understanding, criticism, and evaluation. Serious listening is either selective or concentrated. For someone who listens selectively, the segments of a message fade in and out, while a concentrated listener attends to the entire message. At times you do not need to remember everything that is said. Unfortunately, many listeners do not realize it when they tune out. If we get into a habit of listening half-way, we may find ourselves missing critical material and thus unable to respond effectively.

In social situations, such as parties, coffee breaks, watching television, rock concerts, dinner tables, or talking with friends, we often listen for pleasure and entertainment. Both types of listening are needed in the same conversations. Business associates, family members and friends constantly alter their discussion topics from birdie putts, to Supreme Court decisions about EEOC hiring guidelines to the latest vacation, to the President's new budget cuts. Preparing yourself for all types of listening situations makes you a better communicator.

As one adapts to various purposes of communication, several benefits from effective listening accrue (Barker, 1971).

Listening effectively increases your knowledge and experience. Much information in today's computers or data banks is inaccessible or very difficult to retrieve. By "picking other people's brains," we mean listening to gain a shortcut to knowledge. Asking questions and really listening to the answers gives you information that might take days, weeks, or years to learn by reading books or sitting in front of a computer terminal. Effective listening saves time which translates into saved dollars, time, energy, and productivity.

Recently, a frantic mother called police when her four-month-old daughter was choking. An ambulance was sent, but in the meantime, a police officer described the Heimlich maneuver (in which pressure is applied suddenly below the ribs, forcing air through the throat, dislodging obstructions) by phone. The mother listened well and it worked. Effective listening helped this mother save her child's life.

Time is money, and whereas poor listening is costly, effective listening can result in profits. Consider the numerous times you have benefited through listening. Alert listening helps you pick up hints in business and personal affairs. For example, you may own stock in a textile corporation. While waiting for your stockbroker, you hear her tell a client that the next few months look bad for the textile market. This may be the time for you to sell. Keeping your ears open for "freebies" can give you tips on how to save money as well as decrease your incidence of communication errors.

Better listening means improved work performance. You are in an advantageous position to make decisions when you have all the facts, instructions, and details. One employee complained: "My supervisor never listens to me. Last week, I told him that a big problem was developing. There was no reaction. Then, today, I told his boss the same thing. Even though my supervisor was praised for my being alert, he jumped all over me for not telling him first!" When we fail to listen, we are taking unnecessary chances and may be missing out on the best solutions to problems.

Careful listening helps you learn to hear between the lines. People in sales, for example, often jump to conclusions about what customers want or need. How many times have you had salespersons try to sell you something they wanted you to have rather than what you had come to buy? A business forms salesperson, who was a good listener, recently called on a major airline. He planned to sell ticketing forms, but while talking to the president, he realized he should not push the ticketing forms and sold them personnel forms instead. Three months later, the airline called him to order ticket forms worth nearly a million dollars.

Interpersonal problems can be prevented by listening effectively. Frequently, we talk and act before we really listen. We commit ourselves to decisions that "can't," "don't," or "won't" be carried out. Hasty decisions disappoint family members, associates and customers. Not too long ago, a young woman's car was vandalized while at a body shop. The damage was the responsibility of the body shop where she had left the car for repairs. Before leaving she specifically asked to have the car left inside for extra protection. Evidently, no one listened. The next day, the car's chrome wheels and tires were stolen. Now along with the repairs, the shop had the problem of replacing $800 worth of wheels and tires and soothing an angry customer. Similarly, effective listening helps eliminate communication problems at home. A spouse who "wouldn't mind" going on a company picnic might, from these words, seem noncommittal. However, by listening with all our senses, we would have detected the vocal cues that were saying just the opposite. Listening to both message *content* and *treatment* is critical. Listening with the whole self reduces chances for misunderstanding or later conflict.

SUMMARY

In this chapter, we have stressed the problems caused by inefficient and ineffective listening and why effective listening is critical to communication and personal success. Your awareness of listening problems, their potential costs as well as the rewards, will heighten your overall effectiveness. Some of the benefits include increased knowledge, increased self-confidence, improved performance and productivity, increased enjoyment and decreased tension, and better use of our time.

REFERENCES

Barker, L. L. *Listening Behavior.* Englewood Cliffs, NJ: Prentice-Hall, 1971.

Dietze, A., and Jones, G. Factual memory of secondary school pupils for a short article which they read a single time. *Journal of Educational Psychology,* 1931, 22, 586–98, 667–76.

Learning to Listen. *Corporate Report,* November 1979.

Steil, L. What is your ear-Q? *Cereal Foods World,* March 1975, 20, 136–138.

Steil, L. "What Did You Say?" *Executive's Personal Development Letter,* Alexander Hamilton Institute, Inc., Vol. 6, No. 1, November 1979.

Steil, L. *Your Personal Listening Profile,* Sperry Corporation, 1980.

4
What's Your Ear-Q?

I understand a fury in your words, but not the words.

Shakespeare, Othello, Act IV

A few weeks ago a friend with car trouble called her husband and asked him to pick her up at the corner of Nicollet and Emerson. Half an hour later, she called again. Her daughter said, "Daddy left 30 minutes ago." Later she found that he had gone to Nicollet and Green Acres—not even close. He had recognized Nicollet immediately in her conversation and assumed he knew where she would be without listening to the rest of her instructions. Such daily situations continue to lead to dissatisfaction with our own and others' listening abilities. The first step we'll take in order to deal with this unsatisfactory condition is to develop a personal listening profile.

HOW WELL DO YOU RATE AS A LISTENER?

Listen to yourself and the voices of your world.

The following set of exercises were developed by Lyman K. Steil and are designed to develop a Personal Listening Profile by rating attitudinal and behavioral aspects of your listening practices. The Personal Listening Profile has been completed by thousands of individuals and although there are no correct or incorrect answers, your responses will increase your understanding of yourself as a listener and highlight areas of strength and weakness. After you complete the profile, we'll compare your responses with the average profile of thousands of others.

PERSONAL LISTENING PROFILE

1. Self Analysis

A. Circle the word which best describes you overall as a listener.

Superior Excellent Above average Average Below average Poor Lousy

B. On a scale of 0–100 (100=highest), how would you rate yourself overall as a listener?

73%
_____
(0–100)

C. In your opinion, what four words best describe you overall as a listener?

_____ _____

_____ _____

2. Project Other/Self Analysis

A. TARGET 25: List, by name and relationship, 25 individuals who are most important, or significant, in your life. Do not prioritize or rank-order them; simply list by name and relationship.

1	_____	_____		13	_____	_____
2	_____	_____		14	_____	_____
3	_____	_____		15	_____	_____
4	_____	_____		16	_____	_____
5	_____	_____		17	_____	_____
6	_____	_____		18	_____	_____
7	_____	_____		19	_____	_____
8	_____	_____		20	_____	_____
9	_____	_____		21	_____	_____
10	_____	_____		22	_____	_____
11	_____	_____		23	_____	_____
12	_____	_____		24	_____	_____
				25	_____	_____

B. Once you have completed your identification of the individuals most significant to your life, place them on the following target: five most significant in the bullseye, next five in the next ring, etc.

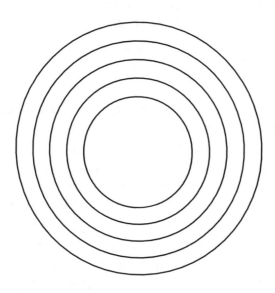

Fig. 4.1 Target 25 Analysis

C. Now how do *you think they would rate you* overall as a listener? (Use the same scale of 0–100.)

Also list four words they would use to describe you as a listener.

(i.e.)

Your best friend	_____	_____
Your boss	_____	_____
A colleague	_____	_____
Job subordinate	_____	_____
Your spouse	_____	_____
Children	_____	_____

3. Other/Self Analysis

A. Repeat your list of Target 25–your significant others.

B. Individually ask each to *rate* and *describe* you overall as a listener. (0–100) (Four Descriptive Words)

4. Self/Other Analysis:

A. Overall, how would you rate (0–100) (Descriptive Words) your significant others?

B. Best listener: Reflect on someone who you would consider to be representative of the *Best Listeners* you have ever known. Identify, rate and describe.

Who _____ 0–100 _____ 4 Descriptive Words
_____

C. Worst listener: Reflect on someone who you would consider to be representative of the *Worst Listeners* you have ever known. Identify, rate, and describe.

Who _____ 0–100 _____ 4 Descriptive Words
_____

Completing these exercises should help to heighten awareness of yourself as a listener and enable you to identify areas where your listening could be improved. (This profile is repeated in Appendix B if you would like to share it with others.) Analysis of part one of this exercise indicates that 90% of all people surveyed fall into the three-point range of above average, average, and below average on the Self-Analysis. We also find that 80% of all listeners rate themselves as average or less. Evaluating your listening behavior may have been difficult for you because of the absence of specific criteria on which to base your decisions. Yet, correctly or incorrectly, with or without criteria or definitions, most people have a perception of themselves as listeners. And the evaluative perception is definable and limited. When other abilities such as golf, black jack, or reading are evaluated, people tend to give a greater variety of answers. A superior golfer would probably break par whenever playing golf, while a terrible black jack player might take a hit on hard twenty (two tens).

It is especially difficult to rate your listening ability numerically. The numerical range for 1B for most people is from 35–85 with an average rating of 55. People rarely rate themselves below 10 or above 90. Typically, of course, scores of 55 on other tests such as driving tests, law boards, or certification exams are failures and have to be repeated.

In Self Analysis 1C the words you used to describe yourself may be positive, negative, or neutral listener characteristics. Of course, words are interpreted differently by different people in various situations. Thinking of yourself as a "critical" listener may have positive meanings for you and negative meanings to someone else. Nevertheless, careful consideration of how you would describe yourself overall as a listener will provide insight and direction for your listening enhancement.

Comparisons of self-rating and projected ratings find most respondents believing that best friends would rate them higher than they rate themselves. In fact, results indicate that best friends would rate you highest as a listener. Why? We can only guess that since best friends are in such intimate, special relationships that you must be a good listener to have this person as a best friend to begin with. People generally think that their bosses would rate them higher than they rated themselves. This may be wishful thinking, but in part is probably accurate. We do tend to listen better to those in authority positions. We listen better out of genuine respect, power need, fear of losing our jobs, or in hopes of promotions.

On average, ratings for colleagues and job subordinates work out almost the same as most people rate themselves or about 55. A dramatic change occurs when we compare our ratings with the projected ratings of spouses. On average, most people feel their spouse would rate them lowest of all. Unless the best friend and the spouse are the same person, the score here is usually significantly lower than the 55 average. Typically, the "projected other" score is 15 percentile points lower than the "self" score. What's particularly interesting is that the figure steadily goes downhill. While newlyweds tend to rate their spouse at the same high level as their best friend, as the marriage continues the ratings drop. So, in households where couples have been married for many years, there may be a lot of talk but no real listening. These descriptions should give you new insights into your listening behavior.

COMMUNICATION CONNECTIONS

It would be difficult for you to remember all the people you've communicated with during the last month. Beyond our Target 25 List, we communicate with hundreds of people in all walks of life from store clerks to beauticians. With some people we communicate several times a day (primary encounters), others several times a month (secondary encounters), and others only occasionally (rare encounters). If you will, list by name the people with whom you have primary, secondary, and rare encounters. (Keep this list in a notebook for future reference.) After listing these people, think about the environment (a street corner, subway, bar, conference, telephone, etc.) in which you communicate. How important is what they have to say? Do they listen well? Do you listen well? Observations of continuing communication interactions often give the best indication of our listening effectiveness.

CAN YOU MAKE YOURSELF LISTEN WELL?

You may be thinking that analyzing the ways we listen to others is fine and good, but it all depends on the situation. You say, "I may not listen well all the time, but when I need to, I do," or "Anybody can listen when they have to!" Most people tend to think that with more effort and concentration they can be effective listeners.

Even though this seems to make sense, in practice most people cannot compel themselves to listen well. Under pressure, many people tense up and are distracted by external factors. Then they blame their listening problems on such things as boring topics, cold rooms, fast speaking rates or a number of other outside distractions. Of course, listeners do face many obstacles, but one of the most influential is the pervasive assumption that effective listening can be willed or automatically turned on. We know listeners can turn listening off with ease, but it can only be turned on to the level to which we have developed our skills. Most important is the fact that with training, your Ear-Q can be improved.

LISTENING EFFICIENCY AND INEFFICIENCY

Listening is not as simple as might be expected. As we noted earlier, most listeners operate on 25% efficiency. Tests show that after a ten-minute oral presentation, the average listener hears, receives, comprehends, and retains only about 50% of the message. After 48 hours, most listeners only remember about 25% of what they heard (Day, 1980; Rasberry, 1980).

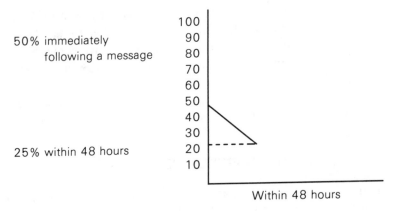

50% immediately
following a message

25% within 48 hours

Within 48 hours

Fig. 5.1 Listening Efficiency and Duration

Think about what you have listened to during the past 48 hours. Of what was said, what did you hear, understand, properly evaluate, remember and respond to appropriately? Probably not as much as you would like. Most people agree that their listening needs improvement and wonder where to begin. Awareness, self-assessment and training is the key. Effective runners begin with stretching exercises; they schedule programs to build strength; and finally after months of preparation reach distance goals of 2 miles, 5 miles, or even 25 miles. Listeners must develop their own individualized training programs.

Most people start each day willing and able to listen, but fail because of the lack of proper training. Before undertaking a listening training program, you first must identify your skills and shortcomings. An old proverb helps describe stages of training development.

"Some men know not, and
Know not that they know not—
    They are fools . . . shun them;

Some men know not, and
Know that they know not—
    They are simple . . . teach them;

Some men know, and
Know not that they know—
      They are asleep . . . wake them;

Some men know, and
Know that they know—
      They are wise men . . . follow them."

Awareness is of primary importance. Without an awareness of your personal skills and weaknesses, you can move no further. You are fortunate; you are already aware of the importance of listening effectiveness. Yet, awareness of the importance of listening is not enough. Thirty years of research shows that others have been aware, but have not changed their listening behavior. Your success depends on the combination of awareness and effort.

SUMMARY

From the Personal Listening Profile, we can obtain a clearer picture of how our listening characteristics compare with others. We have learned that without proper training, we typically don't listen well. Our listening efficiency is approximately 50 percent immediately after a message and about 25 percent 48 hours later. This is one reason that listeners are often ineffective. However, we also know that with awareness and effort, listening can be improved. The next chapter explains typical listener strengths and weaknesses.

REFERENCES

Day, C. How do you rate as a listener? *Industry Week.* April 1980.

Rasberry, R. W. Are Your Students Listening? A method for putting listening instruction into the business communication course. *Proceedings.* Southwest American Business Communication Association Spring Conference, 1980, 215.

5

Identifying Your Personal Listening Strengths and Weaknesses *Good & Bad listening skills 10. problems*

I can't help hearing, but I don't always listen.

George Burns as God in *Oh God*

A supervisor in charge of a large group of clerical personnel held office meetings on Friday afternoons. Recently the supervisor began calling these meetings twice a week. A frustrated group of employees got together and wrote a memo complaining about wasted time in so many meetings. The next morning a memo was placed on each of their desks, "Poor listening causes MEETINGS!"

With an understanding of the importance of listening to overall communication success, you now need to identify your individual listening strengths and weaknesses. Before you do, remember you listen the way you do (effectively or not) because of years of practice. Listening is a learned behavior. It is also habitual. Most important, you *can* learn to improve your listening effectiveness by building on your strengths and eliminating your weaknesses.

CHARACTERISTICS OF EFFECTIVE AND INEFFECTIVE LISTENERS

In 1948, the "Father of Listening," Dr. Ralph Nichols, identified characteristics of effective and ineffective listeners (Nichols, 1948). Dr. Nichols's discoveries of 30 years ago have continued to be studied with no significant differences being found between the good and poor listeners of 30 years ago and those of today. Good listeners are typically categorized as:

Alert	Caring
Responsive	Attending
Patient	Other-centered
Non-interrupting	Curious
Empathic	Effective Evaluator
Interested	Non-emotional
Understanding	Not Distracted

Poor listeners on the other hand are often categorized as:

Inattentive	Self-centered
Defensive	Uncaring
Impatient	Quick to judge
Interrupting	Distracted
Disinterested	Apathetic
Insensitive	Emotional

Certainly there are numerous other ways to categorize good and poor listeners. As an interesting exercise, ask ten friends, family members, co-workers, or acquaintances to each think of 10 words that describe the best listener and 10 words that describe the worst listener they have ever known.

Make a collective list and you will have a productive compilation to compare yourself to.

You probably recognize characteristics of your listening behavior from the foregoing columns or compiled lists. For further individual analysis of your listening skills, complete the following exercise.

HOW WELL DO YOU LISTEN?

Analysis of Your Bad Listening Habits

How often do you indulge in ten almost universal bad listening habits? Check yourself carefully on each one:

HABIT	FREQUENCY					SCORE
	Almost always	Usually	Some-times	Seldom	Almost never	
1. Calling the subject uninteresting	_____	_____	_____	_____	_____	_____
2. Criticizing the speaker's delivery	_____	_____	_____	_____	_____	_____
3. Getting *over* stimulated by some point within the speech	_____	_____	_____	_____	_____	_____
4. Listening only for facts	_____	_____	_____	_____	_____	_____
5. Trying to outline everything	_____	_____	_____	_____	_____	_____
6. Faking attention to the speaker	_____	_____	_____	_____	_____	_____

7. Tolerating or creating distractions _____ _____ _____ _____ _____ | _____

8. Avoiding difficult expository material _____ _____ _____ _____ _____ | _____

9. Letting emotion-laden words arouse personal antagonism _____ _____ _____ _____ _____ | _____

10. Wasting the advantage of thought speed _____ _____ _____ _____ _____ |

Total _____

TOTAL SCORE INTERPRETATION: Below 70— You need training.
From 79–90—You listen well. Above 90—You are extraordinarily good.

For every "Almost always" checked, give yourself a score of	2
For every "Usually" checked, give yourself a score of	4
For every "Sometimes" checked, give yourself a score of	6
For every "Seldom" checked, give yourself a score of	8
For every "Almost never" checked, give yourself a score of	10

How does your score compare with your earlier rating from 0 to 100 (Chapter 4:1. Self Analysis)? The average score on this latest exercise is 62 compared to an average of 55 in 1. Self Analysis. It should have helped to break listening into specific areas of competence. Before examining each of these listening problems in detail, we need to look at factors which may influence your listening effectiveness.

FACTORS THAT INHIBIT LISTENING SUCCESS

How would you feel knowing that a jury would forget 75 percent of the information presented in your behalf? As we stated earlier, most people listen at rates of 25 percent effectiveness. Listening can be improved, but listening problems are different from other types of problems because you may not be aware that the problem exists. Four factors which inhibit listening are related to your mental state.

First, it is difficult to focus on what is being said when we have personal and or professional problems. Having an argument with your spouse before leaving for work takes much of your energy, and distracts analyzing what went wrong. Inner conflicts such as this make it difficult to concentrate when listening.

A second factor which inhibits listening is general anxiety. Inner conflict usually stimulates or increases your general anxiety. If you are concerned about an IRS audit, for example, or a shipment reaching its destination on time, or if you're being considered for promotion, you may find it difficult to listen to others. Regardless of the cause, anxiety causes you to lose attention and energy necessary to listen effectively.

A third inhibiting factor is a closed mind. It is difficult to tell whether or not we have closed minds because of our "filtering agents," which influence our perceptions. It is easy to be open-minded on issues we agree with, but controversial issues are more difficult. Look at your attitudes, opinions and beliefs to see if you have tendencies to turn people off by not seeing another side of the issue.

One of the most serious inhibitors of effective listening is trying to do too many things at once. Effective listening requires full-time attention. It is frustrating to you and to others if during a conversation, you talk on the phone, sign letters, wave to secretaries, or doodle on a notepad. Setting aside other tasks while in conversation will improve your ability to listen. The last portion of this chapter is devoted to analyzing poor listening habits. As you read, try to ask yourself "Am I guilty of this?"

INFLUENTIAL LISTENING CHARACTERISTICS

"There is no such thing as an uninteresting subject. There are only uninterested people."
G. K. Chesterton

While examining your lists of good and poor listener characteristics, you may begin to see characteristics in yourself, other speakers, messages and environments which affect your listening ability and comprehension. Research has helped to identify internal and external variables which may influence your listening behavior. Many of these variables operate as distractions and will be discussed in greater detail later. We need to keep in mind that research data, when interpreted, is subject to human inadequacies and biases.

Listener Characteristics

Our personal characteristics and prior experiences affect our ability to listen. Many observers question the listening differences between males and females. Numerous investigations (Brandon, 1956; Farrow, 1963; Lundsteen, 1963; Nichols, 1951; Caffrey, 1955) have resulted in conflicting conclusions regarding the impact of physical gender on listening. Weaver (1972) suggests that scores on listening tests may only reflect *differences* between sexes and not the *quality* of listening. Simply put, we note that males and females score differently as listeners, and that such differences should not lead to interpretations of superiority/inferiority. With societal changes impacting on both males and females, listening attitudes and behaviors could be expected to show subtle shifts over time.

Research has also attempted to find out if there are relationships between age and listening ability. Age of listener research indicates a relationship between the listener's age and listening comprehension which is slight to moderate in degree (Steil, 1977). It has however been reported that younger children "have considerably shorter attention spans than young adults. Similarly, when a person reaches old age and senility, . . . listening may be affected negatively" (Barker, 1971).

Personality has also been found to affect listening ability (Stromer, 1955). Ego involvement tends to reduce listener comprehension, while objectivity tends to increase listener comprehension. In addition, listeners who have personal worries or feelings of insecurity, or feel they are "doomed to failure" also tend to be poorer listeners than those who are optimistic and free from worry.

A characteristic that is related to personality is *listener apprehension*. People with high levels of listener apprehension have a tendency to respond to listening situations with anxiety. This anxiety reduces comprehension and retention of information. A few years ago the Receiver Apprehension Test (RAT) was introduced to measure trait listening anxiety (Wheeless, 1975). Recent results using the RAT suggest that receiver apprehension is related to inadequate information processing and cognitive complexity. The degree to which individuals are afraid of misinterpreting, inadequately processing, or adjusting to information affects how they listen (Scott and Wheeless, 1977). Listening failures in the past seem to compound the problem. Additional research has found relationships between cognitive complexity and receiver apprehension. People who process information more efficiently have less listener apprehension (Beatty and Payne, 1981).

Intelligence factors and their impact on listening have been investigated by many researchers. To summarize the relationship, it has been noted that it is obvious that any mental activity—including listening—depends to a certain extent on intelligence. Yet such research indicates a positive, but not high, relationship (Barker, 1971).

Speaker Characteristics

Besides variables you have as a listener, your listening ability is also influenced by speaker variables. For a short period of time a knowledgeable individual can comprehend a technical report on nuclear power reactors delivered at a rapid speaking rate (perhaps 400 words per minute), but for longer time periods it is difficult to listen at a rate above normal (165 wpm) without training (Goodman-Malamuth II, 1956). The best speaking rate is dependent on the message content, knowledge level of the audience, length of message, and conditions under which listening is to occur. Along with the rate, research also suggests that it is easier for audiences to listen to more fluent (using fewer vocal pauses: uh, and um) speakers (Barker, Watson, and Kibler, 1982).

The visibility of a speaker also seems to improve listening ability (Gauger, 1951). As mentioned earlier, many meanings are transmitted through nonverbal cues. Through facial expressions speakers not only add interest to their messages, but also change the meanings of their words. Research also indicates that gestures are another form of nonverbal behavior which serves to influence listening (Haiman, 1949). The more gestures speakers use, the more information that listeners comprehend. Other speaker qualities that affect listening include: the speaker's reputation, how well a speaker is liked, and whether or not the speaker can be heard adequately.

Message Characteristics

What we hear a speaker say also affects our ability to listen (Berlo and Gulley, 1957). Our personal values may influence our ability to understand a message without our even being aware of it. Research suggests that we comprehend more information when our values are in agreement with what is being discussed. However, there is a tendency for us to listen more carefully to a message that we strongly disagree with than to those messages we don't feel as strongly about. One reason for this may be that we often attempt to find points of weakness. Yet if we do find and focus on a weakness, our ability to listen to the rest of the message decreases.

Environmental Characteristics

Listening ability is affected by variables in the listener, the speaker, the message, and the environment. Sometimes we fail to adjust for environmental factors that may interfere with our listening (Nichols, 1948). Rooms that are well ventilated and that have comfortable temperature settings are more conducive to effective listening. Can you remember what it was like listening to a commencement speaker on a hot day in June? Where you sit can also affect your listening effectiveness. The closer people sit to each other the more likely they are to listen carefully; whereas the people who sit further away tend to listen less effectively.

Other environmental factors that influence listening behavior include family circumstances. Research indicates that children raised without brothers or sisters tend to comprehend better than children from large families. An only child is used to being listened to and also to listening with little external interference, while children in large families are bombarded by large numbers of messages and learn to (and need to) screen out some messages. Children that are raised in homes where more than one language is spoken often listen less effectively than children in one-language homes. The use of two languages causes confusion and it takes time for a child to understand and use both languages properly. In addition to factors which influence our listening ability, we need to look at ways in which listening is inhibited.

THE TEN WORST LISTENING PROBLEMS

It is often easier to identify undesirable listening traits in others than to see them in oneself. While examining the following poor listening habits, try to recall situations in which another person is engaged in the habit. If you recognize the behavior in someone else, next take a critical look at your own listening behavior.

Viewing a Topic as Uninteresting

Most of us have been forced to attend meetings that were either mandatory or "strongly recommended." It may have been a stockholders' meeting, a training seminar, your boss's "state of the office" report, or a speech by your spouse's favorite author. Do you remember how you behaved as a listener? Chances are if you forced yourself to listen through the first part, your interest increased (at least minimally) and you learned more than you would have thought. There is a tendency for us to prejudge topics and situations as boring, unimportant, dull or dry. We develop a "who cares" attitude and quickly turn off the speaker or only half listen. When we tune out messages, we will not readily follow, effectively evaluate, or retain much of what was presented. In addition, we tend to reinforce our negative attitudes about the topic.

Skilled listeners search for areas of interest. At first they too may want to turn off the speaker, but good listeners quickly adjust their listening mode to match the situation. Time is a precious commodity and if you are forced by circumstances beyond your control to spend time in a communication situation where you can listen actively or passively, it seems reasonable that you would try to make the best use of your time. You may believe that mentally "blocking out" a message so that you can think about more important matters is a better use of time. At times however, a communication situation has potential for providing something you can use in the future.

Effective listeners know how to pick out the critical moments in listening situations which offer the most value. In particular, good listeners know how to spot the important aspects of meetings and lectures. When forced to attend meetings, it sometimes is a good idea to creatively make the best use of your time by working on other projects (mentally) until the information critical to you is discussed. Part of you must act as a monitoring device so that you do not miss valuable information.

It is important to point out that selectively listening for the most valuable moment is not appropriate for all situations. Half listening to a spouse or boss can get you into difficulty, especially if you fail to listen to all of a message because you felt that you already knew what was going to be said. Sometimes we must force ourselves to listen actively when interpersonal relationships may be affected.

Good listeners have a constructively selfish attitude. They look for valuable uses and possibilities that can be derived from each topic and situation. Remember even though critical value moments have a place in listening we still must be wary of dismissing situations prematurely by calling the subject uninteresting.

Criticizing the Speaker's Delivery

Think for a moment about meetings you've attended. What speakers stood out in your mind? We often remember some aspect of their delivery or appearance rather than what was actually said. Our attention is quickly diverted by speakers who look at the floor while talking, speak in a monotone, play with objects, or wear clothes that do not match. Speakers need to be aware that visual aspects of their delivery negatively and positively affect untrained listeners. Good listeners however try to overlook or repress negative aspects of a speaker's delivery which may interfere with the message.

Since there is a tendency to remember the delivery rather than the message, effective listening requires us to focus on the content of what is said. Generally, the value of what we listen to is in the content, not in the delivery. We don't need to remember what the speaker's clothing, gestures, posture, or facial expressions were. As effective listeners, we must disregard negative or novel elements in a speaker's delivery or physical appearance that might divert our attention.

Getting Overstimulated by Some Point in the Speech

When we are ego-involved with subjects that are being discussed, we usually let our emotions take control. When we disagree with a speaker's view, there is a tendency for us to make internal refutations or rehearse a response while the speaker is delivering the message. For example, a delegate from the school bus driver's association tells the board of education that the drivers will strike unless they receive pay increases. Unless the members of the board are good listeners, they will have a tendency to react emotionally to the remainder of the speaker's message. This emotional involvement may distort or interfere with their acquisition of important information which follows.

In Chapter 7, we will discuss ways to control the tendency to create emotional "deaf" spots with respect to what the speaker says. For now, we point out the need for witholding judgment until the entire message has been heard. We need to fully receive and understand first so that our judgment and responses will be appropriate later.

Listening Only for Facts

Our educational careers have conditioned us to take notes in order to pass examinations. In addition, our work and daily lives have conditioned us to be preoccupied with "facts." This conditioning process creates a type of listener who listens primarily for factual information that can be recorded on paper (to be reviewed and used later). Obviously, there are times when it is important to listen just for facts (e.g., time to pick up payroll checks, the number of copies needed, the due date of the paper, or the list of errands that need to be completed before the office picnic). At other times, listening only for facts can be disadvantageous. The major problem promoted by this practice of listening only for facts is a tendency to avoid critical analysis and evaluation of the message while listening. If the message is full of symbolism or multiple interpretations, the practice of listening primarily for facts may produce a distorted version of the message. We get into the habit of Joe Friday, of "Dragnet" fame who said, "Just the facts, Ma'am the facts!"

Good listeners try to analyze the communication setting, the purpose, intent, structure, and the nature of the message. If facts are important, we listen for them, but if it is more important to interpret and analyze the message, we do not listen just for facts. When you evaluate the message, you increase your chances of remembering the facts too, because you have a better understanding of how all the parts fit into the complete message.

Trying to Outline Everything

Another habit we have acquired, primarily from our educational experiences, is trying to outline everything we hear as we would in notetaking. This tendency to organize using an outline is sometimes effective, unless the speaker has a different organizational pattern, or no organizational pattern at all. As listeners we should be careful not to impose our own organizational pattern on the speaker. If we superimpose an outline on the speaker's message, it is possible that our notes will be misleading and cause problems for us later on. Other problems occur when you try to take down everything you hear or don't review what you've written down later. (Chapter 8 presents hints on notetaking.)

Rather than attempting to outline the message point by point, good listeners listen for a few minutes and then jot down key ideas and concepts. Search the message mentally for important points, and then try to avoid getting caught up in extended examples. The best listeners: take notes; adapt to the organizational structure of the speaker; and use the notes later on.

Faking Attention to the Speaker

When was the last time you pretended to listen when your mind was actually miles away? At times certain thoughts race through your mind which are so interesting or important that you cannot force yourself to listen to a speaker. In these cases, we often pretend to listen because of embarrassment or fear of punishment from superiors. We use fake facial expressions, eye contact, and head nods to signal others that we are listening even if we are not interested in what they have to say. A failure to show interest may cause problems. We hope that the speaker is not aware that we're not listening to what he or she says. At other times, we take "mental trips" without realizing we've gone anywhere. A word or phrase gets our mind thinking about food, summer vacations, or an appointment. We snap back to reality, usually after only a few seconds, but a lot of information can be lost.

During World War II Hitler became aware of the "mental trip" listening problem. Since he wanted all German people to listen and respond to his radio broadcasts, marshalls were set up in neighborhoods to make sure that the masses tuned in. He still had no assurance that people were listening so in order to insure attention his marshalls quizzed the public periodically. If they failed to answer the questions correctly or unfavorably, they were reported and punished. Most speakers want us to listen to and not just hear what is said. Faking attention usually serves to reinforce the speaker, but you as the listener are not being sincere. Problems arise when faking becomes a *real* habit. When you are habituated to faking attention you may not be aware of what you are doing. If you often find yourself not remembering what the speaker has said, check yourself to see if you have been practicing this habit subconsciously. Remember, for communication success, we each need to pass the 51% minimum responsibility test.

Tolerating or Creating Distractions

When we think of communication distractions, we may think of elementary children disrupting classes by throwing spitballs or shooting rubber bands. However, we all cause and/or tolerate distractions in all our communication activities. At home we leave the television on while talking at the dinner table, at work we turn our desks to be able to see what is happening in the hallway or outer offices, and at parties we try to greet everyone while talking to a long lost friend.

Some distractions such as soft music being played in the background, outside noise, movement around us, or similar physical distractions cannot be controlled in our environments. The new modular open office spaces are a prime example of an environment in which numerous distractions are always present. Employees have to deal with the sound of typewriters, telephones, conversations, normal traffic in and out, etc. Failure to adjust to, or compensate for, such distractions is a common listening problem. If you cannot modify the external environment conditions, you must modify your own internal listening behavior in order to take in messages directed toward you. Remember the first step to minimize your personal distractions is to identify them. Specific methods to help you control them will be discussed in Chapter 6.

Avoiding Difficult Material

Listeners often tend to avoid messages that are difficult to understand. This tendency is similar to the habit of calling a subject uninteresting prematurely. Again, because of demands on your mental energy, you may tend to ignore or avoid what a speaker has to say. Especially in business, instead of listening to what has been said, there is a tendency to wait for a written report. Many people would rather avoid listening to "Meet the Press" or presidential speeches and buy a newspaper or weekly magazine with a condensed version or synopsis of an issue.

There are times when we need to listen to relaxing material (soap operas, television comedies, etc.), but our ears need practice for more difficult listening situations. The tendency to tune out difficult material may cause problems at work, since it is necessary to listen even when you are not strongly motivated. If you find yourself frequently avoiding difficult listening, try to modify your behavior. A key question is: What do you listen to? Good listeners seek out difficult and complex listening situations.

Letting Emotionally Laden Words Arouse Personal Antagonism

This poor listening habit is similar to overreacting to some idea presented by the speaker; however, in this particular instance, listeners react to specific words rather than the broader concept expressed in the message. Poor listeners are generally unaware of these hot spots or "emotional triggers" that arouse their emotions. Words such as "Gun Control," "Abortion," "Right Wing," or "Left Wing," and "profanity" tend to have emotional connotations built into them. Regardless of their context, such words often trigger what are called "signal reactions." In other words, we react to the words and not their intended meanings. Ways to avoid reactions to emotionally laden words are discussed in Chapter 7. Skilled listeners come to know themselves well enough so that they can overcome the spontaneous response to their "trigger" words. They focus on what the speaker says and withold judgment while the speaker continues. By knowing the speakers, words, and subjects that trigger your emotions, you will be in a better position to control your communication situations and their results.

Wasting the Advantage of Thought Speed

For some time, it has been known that we can think at a rate of over 400 words a minute, but speakers rarely talk at a rate of over 175 words a minute. This thought–speed/ speech–speed differential must be taken into consideration, otherwise the listener's mind may run ahead of the speaker. Because of this extra time, we often prepare to answer questions or points before fully understanding them. We think we know what the speaker is going to say and begin formulating

mental or oral questions with regard to the message, or perhaps a "great comeback." This habit can make listeners appear rude, foolish, or not very bright. Be careful that you do
not mentally jump so far ahead of the speaker, and begin to
answer questions you think he is going to ask, that you miss
part of his message.

The same problem relates to other areas of listening.
Sometimes we develop listening habits that distract us from
what the speaker is saying. Many listeners go off on so-called
"mental trips." Constructive or destructive use of the time-
rate differential often makes the difference between good and
bad listeners. Good listeners use the time advantageously to
evaluate, anticipate, review, and summarize what has been
said.

In addition, there are other methods for enhancing your
thought/speech speed advantage. You have, at times, listened
to lectures or conversations, or news programs in which you
thought the speaker was running on "slow." You may have
wanted to push the person's speech–speed button to "fast;"
to pull the words from his or her mouth; or, to say "Get to
the point!" Unfortunately in most situations, we have little
control over the speaker's speech speed.

In recent years, educators and researchers have focused
on finding methods of enhancing the available thought-speed
advantage through the use of *compressed speech*. Compressed
speech shortens the time required by increasing the number
of words spoken per minute (Weaver, 1972). The results have
been encouraging. Normal speech has been compressed by 50
percent (282 wpm) without loss of comprehension (Fairbanks, Guttman, and Miron, 1957; Reid, 1968; Steil, 1976).
Thus, with compression and listener development, oral messages can be listened to in substantially less time without significant loss of comprehension. Some people question the use
of compressed speech, but researchers have found that most
people actually prefer faster speaking rates. In fact, many
blind people had been using a form of compressed speech for
years, by increasing the speed at which their records are
played. With the advanced state-of-the-art technology for

speech compression developed by VSC (Variable Speech Control) company of San Francisco, listeners who choose to listen more efficiently are able to save time and increase their retention.

Of course, the listening problems we have been discussing are not exhaustive and many overlap each other. However, these are among the more persistent listening problems, since they were identified by Dr. Nichols nearly 35 years ago. If you recognize habits similar to these which hinder your listening effectiveness, first try to become sensitive to them. Awareness of the problems will assist you toward avoiding them in the future. The following chart provides a partial summary of the points and suggests some "checks" to help you analyze your own listening problems and strengths.

TEN KEYS TO EFFECTIVE LISTENING

Following is a list of guidelines to better listening. These practices are in fact, a program for developing better listening habits that could last a lifetime.

Ten Keys to Effective Listening	The Bad Listener	The Good Listener
1. Find areas of interest.	Tunes out dry subjects.	Looks for benefits and opportunities; asks "What's in it for me?"
2. Judge content, not delivery.	Tunes out if delivery is poor.	Judges content; skips over delivery errors.
3. Hold your fire.	Tends to enter into argument.	Doesn't judge until message is complete.
4. Listen for ideas.	Listens for facts.	Listens for central themes.

5. Be flexible.	Takes intensive notes using only one system.	Takes fewer notes; uses several different systems, depending on speaker.
6. Work at listening.	Shows no energy output. Attention is faked.	Works hard, exhibits active body state.
7. Resist distractions.	Distracted easily.	Fights or avoids distractions; tolerates bad habits; knows how to concentrate.
8. Exercise your mind.	Resists difficult, expository material; seeks light, recreational material.	Uses heavier material as exercise for the mind.
9. Keep your mind open.	Reacts to emotional words.	Interprets color words; does not get hung up on them.
10. Capitalize on the fact that *thought* is faster than *speech*.	Tends to daydream with slow speakers.	Challenges, anticipates, mentally summarizes; weighs the evidence; listens between the lines to tone of voice.

Identifying your listening strengths and weaknesses is the first step toward improving your listening success. The next three chapters are the "how to do it" chapters on improving your listening. Many of the ideas are "common sense" suggestions, which you may have thought of before, yet they are included because we often forget or neglect to use them in our listening. These suggestions should stimulate your thinking and help you to find additional common sense suggestions which directly relate to your personal listening behavior during family, work, and social interactions.

Remember, active listening takes energy and work. For you to gain the most from reading the next few chapters, you must *apply* the principles. It is relatively easy to identify a variety of solutions to a problem. However, implementing the best solution is a more difficult matter. How often have you come up with a great idea that failed because it was not carried out? Just as ideas cannot work until all the steps have been completed, listening improvement cannot occur until the suggestions are practiced in actual listening situations.

Before looking at specific suggestions for listening improvement, there are two general points that need to be stressed. The first is the need to constantly remind yourself that listening is vital to communication and your personal communication success. Second, you should periodically refer back to the poor listening habits in this chapter (see page 57) to modify or correct those habits that have appeared in your listening behavior.

SPECIFIC SUGGESTIONS FOR LISTENING IMPROVEMENT

The following suggestions can be applied to all types of listening situations. While reading the rest of this book, try to keep these in mind as tips and techniques are given for dealing with distractions, emotions, message structures, and message evaluations and responses. First, *prepare* and *commit yourself to active listening.* Effective listening includes the matter of "psyching up" yourself to a state of psychological and physical readiness. As professional athletes prepare their minds and bodies for competition in sports, we need to train and condition for effective listening.

Second, *try to think about the topic and situation in advance.* Remember, you need to be a "selfish listener." Find ways to make the topic vital and rewarding to you. Look for the "value moments." When you are somewhat familiar with a topic, later learning is more efficient and longer lasting. When you think about topics, words, or people that distract you, you will be able to anticipate and overcome them.

Third, *concentrate and try not to let your thoughts wander.* Each of us takes "mental trips" while listening. A speaker mentions how oil prices have affected airline travel and before you even realize it, you may be thinking about your last business trip, a vacation to Hawaii, or that you'd like to take flying lessons. It sometimes takes effort to stay with the speaker throughout the entire message.

Fourth, *plan to report the general essence of what you are listening to to someone else later.* A commitment to report to another person will force you to change your listening behavior. You can't report what you haven't listened to earlier. At first, this is difficult, but eventually you will be able to condense a 20–30 minute message into a 3 or 4 minute overview.

Fifth, *take notes, but adapt your notetaking to the speaker, topic, organizational structure, and situation.* Of course, review your notes later and add to them for maximum development. Practice your notetaking in controlled situations (i.e., classes, church, news broadcasts, business meetings, conferences, and conventions.)

SUMMARY

This chapter is designed to help you pinpoint some of your personal listening strengths and weaknesses. Completing the "How Well Do You Listen" exercise gives you a checklist of areas in which you can begin to improve your listening habits. Listener, speaker, message, and environmental variables may influence our ability to listen. Sometimes we fail to understand how mental states such as inner conflict, general anxiety, closed-mindedness, and trying to do too many things at once affect listening effectiveness. Our listening habits are learned, as we saw in our discussion of ten of the most frequent listening problems. To help you deal with them more effectively, we considered ten keys to effective listening. In the next chapter we will discuss specific factors which influence your listening sucess.

REFERENCES

Barker, L. L. *Listening Behavior.* Englewood Cliffs, NJ: Prentice-Hall, 1971.

Barker, L. L., Watson, K. W., and the late Kibler, R. J. An investigation of the effect of presentations by effective and ineffective speakers on listening. Paper presented to the International Listening Association Convention, Washington, D.C., 1982.

Beatty, M. J. and Payne S. K. Receiver apprehension and cognitive complexity *Western Journal of Speech Communication,* 1981, **45**, 363–69.

Berlo, D. and Gulley, H. Some determinants of the effect of and communication in producing attitude change and learning. *Speech Monographs,* 1957, **24**, 14–18.

Brendon, J. An experimental TV study: the relative effectiveness of presenting factual information by the lecture, interviews, and discussion methods. *Speech Monographs,* 1956, **22**, 272–83.

Brown C. Studies in Listening Comprehension. *Speech Monographs,* 1959, **25**, 288–94.

Caffrey J. A. *Review of Educational Research,* April 1955, **25**, 121–38.

Erickson, A. An analysis of several factors in an experimental study of listening at the college level. Unpublished doctoral dissertation, University of Oregon, Eugene, Oregon, 1954.

Fairbanks, G., Guttman, N., and Miron, M. S. Auditory comprehension in relation to listening rate and selective verbal redundancy. *Journal of Speech and Hearing Disorders,* 1957, **22**, 23.

Gauger, P. The effect of gesture and the presence or absence of the speaker on the listening comprehension of 11th and 12th grade high school pupils. Unpublished doctoral dissertation, University of Wisconsin, Madison, Wisconsin, 1951.

Goodman-Malamuth II, L. An experimental study of the effects of rate of speaking upon listenability. Unpublished doctoral dissertation, University of Southern California, Los Angeles, 1956.

Haiman, F. An experimental study of the effect of ethos on public speaking. *Speech Monographs,* September 1949, **16**, 190–202.

Nichols, R. Factors accounting for differences in comprehension of materials presented orally in the classroom. Unpublished doctoral dissertation, State University of Iowa, Iowa City, 1948.

Reid, R. Grammatical complexity and comprehension of compressed speech. *Journal of Communication,* 1968, **18**, 236.

Scott, M. D. and Wheeless, L. R. The relationship of three types of communication apprehension to classroom achievement, *Southern Speech Communication Journal,* 1977, **42**, 246–55.

Steil, L. K. Compressed Speech — Another Educational Tool: Boon or Bane? *Toward Better Teaching,* Fall 1975, Vol. 9, No. 1.

Steil, L. K. A Longitudinal Analysis of Listening Pedagogy in Minnesota Secondary Public Schools. Unpublished doctoral dissertation, Wayne State University, Detroit, Michigan, 1977.

Stromer, W. Listening and personality. *Education,* January 1955, **75**, 322–26.

Weaver, C. H. *Human Listening: Process and Behavior.* Indianapolis: Bobbs-Merrill, 1972.

Wheeless, L. R. An investigation of receiver apprehension and social context dimensions of communication apprehension. *The Speech Teacher,* 1975, **24**, 258–68.

6
Identifying and Dealing with Distractions

Listening is a rare happening among human beings. You cannot listen to the word another is speaking if you are preoccupied with your appearance, or with impressing the other, or are trying to decide what you are going to say when the other stops talking, or are debating about whether what is being said is true or relevant or agreeable. Such matters have their place, but only after listening to the word as the word is being uttered.
Listening is a primitive act of love in which a person gives himself to another's word, making himself accessible and vulnerable to that word.

William Stringfellow *Friend's Journal*

We live in a world of disruptive influences that block effective and accurate communication. Most interferences go relatively unnoticed and people generally are not aware that their listening is adversely affected. Distractions occur and affect us at all levels and in every situation. We are constantly interrupted by telephone calls, appointment schedules, employee traffic, correspondence, meetings and deadlines. Many secretaries minimize distractions for bosses by screening calls, sending sales personnel to other departments, and controlling the day's agenda. Unless you become aware of and skilled at combatting interfering forces, distractions can destroy your ability to listen.

SHORT-TERM AND LONG-TERM MEMORY

Think about the number of times you have driven to the grocery store and had to call home to ask what you were to buy, or forgotten a joke until someone started telling it, or remembered a message you were to give someone too late after seeing them. Our memory, like our listening, is affected by internal and external distractions. For this reason, many people think of listening and memory interchangeably. At times, however, we may listen very carefully and still not remember something a few minutes later. By considering some of the differences between short-term and long-term memory, we may see the relationship between listening and memory.

Short-term memory operates when information is used immediately. Research suggests that information is forgotten in 30 seconds without some type of rehearsal such as repeating what was said or read (Shiffrin and Atkinson, 1969). Thirty seconds is not unduly long for us to retain information. Yet, think about situations in which you have forgotten a phone number after looking it up in the directory, a person's name shortly after being introduced, a phone message after hanging up, or instructions immediately after receiving them.

Short-term memory is associated with a rapid forgetting rate; moreover, it is also easily disrupted. Questions and/or comments made during conversations that are not relevant to the important information often causes people to forget the main points. The amount of information retained is limited in short-term memory. After hearing a series of numbers, list of items, or list of names, we have a limited capacity with regard to how much of the given information we can repeat later (Lefrancois, 1975).

Long-term memory, on the other hand, is what we rely on most heavily. Information learned in school, special vacations, activities you participated in while growing up, and songs, are types of information that are stored in long-term memory. Long-term memory is relatively unaffected by activity before and after an event.

Think about how good you feel when a one-time acquaintance remembers your name. Our names are very important to us, but how often have we forgotten a name after just being introduced or avoided someone whose name slipped our mind. Probably more often than we would like to admit. Even though remembering a person's name is a way of acknowledging their importance and individuality, many listeners get distracted during introductions to others.

It would seem to be very simple to catch at least a first or last name during an introduction, but so much happens during that first few minutes of an encounter that many of us don't. As mentioned earlier, our short-term memory forgets in about 30 seconds without a rehearsal. Most of us don't give ourselves time to rehearse during introductions because we are too busy thinking about what we are going to say, how we look, if we will come across well, how the other person looks, or some other aspect of the situation. Thinking about yourself often works to your disadvantage during introductions, especially when you make a negative impression by forgetting the person's name later.

Since our names are so important, the following keys to remembering names should help you with future introductions (Lorayne, 1975).

1. Be sure you hear the name.

2. Try to spell the name.

3. Make a remark about the name.

4. Use the name during the initial conversation.

5. Use the name when you leave.

A special occasion such as a first date may be anticipated and the memories retained indefinitely by deliberate effort.

Long-term memory is not limited like short-term memory. People easily remember information that goes back to their early childhood. Although recalling particular dates, names or cities may be slower and more difficult in later years, the information is often still "on the tip of our tongue."

IMPROVING SHORT-TERM MEMORY

As we have seen, we ordinarily have the most difficulty with short-term memory. Before messages are stored in our memories, we first have to listen to the information. The following suggestions should help you improve your short-term memory (Lefrancois, 1975).

1. Pay attention to the information received. (Make sure that you can hear and see well.)

2. Repeat the information. (If necessary, take written notes.)

3. Reduce interference by using the information immediately. (Dial the number before doing anything else.)

Of course, our memory, both short- and long-term, is irrelevant if we do not first *sense,* or get the speaker's message. Although we can, and often do, forget what we have heard, it is of course obvious that we cannot remember that which we have never heard. Thus, let's examine the negative impact of distractions on listening.

DISTRACTIONS

Let's consider two types of distractions: internal and external. Internal distracitons are influenced by your inner psychological states. Tension about a company merger, eating too much at lunch, having a head cold, getting only four hours of sleep, or the death of a close friend influences how you listen. External distractions are all around us and are usually not under our conscious control. Outside noises such as traffic or lawn mowers, interruptions by phone or personal visits, the physical environment, visual stimuli such as low cut dresses or hairy chests, physical mannerisms, or vocal characteristics such as dialects and professional jargon may adversely influence your listening behavior.

Internal and external distractions can function independently or in combination with each other. For example, let's say your daughter's teacher made an appointment to see you at 4:30 on a Friday afternoon. You arrive in a lousy mood after fighting traffic, not eating lunch, and losing a major account. On top of all your internal frustrations, the school's air conditioning system is broken, workers are hammering, children are playing in the room and a bell rings. Situations like this will understandably hinder your listening effectiveness. Some of these distractions may seem insurmountable, but with conscious effort and practice, you will develop the skill needed to overcome these and other distractions you face every day.

In Chapter 4, we considered the difficulty of willing yourself to listen. As we have seen, if you are listening effectively, you should hear what is said (sensing), correctly understand it (interpreting), determine whether it is important to remember (evaluating), and be able to retrieve it for later use (responding). If you did have trouble with listening, it is probably because you were distracted. You could have been interrupted, you may have felt that it wasn't important, or perhaps you said to yourself, "I give up, there are too many facts." Many of our distractions are self-induced and we fail to sense the message at all. If you never sense a message, you won't be able to deal with it at each higher level.

An analogy can be made between missing information when listening, and going fishing. If while fishing in a stream, you miss the first fish that go by, what do you do? Do you wade downstream after them? Of course not—you try for the next fish to come along. If you stand there thinking about the fish that got away, you'll probably miss the next fish, too. The same is true with listening. If you sit there thinking about the information that you missed, you will probably miss the next bit of information too. You need to come back later and deal with what you missed. Don't let it become another interference and because of it let all the information (fish) get away.

Are You Tested on Distractions?

Occasionally we tell ourselves that some distractions are important, but are they? If they are, can you remember a time that you had to recall or report on distractions, on interference? Clearly, no. You are seldom, if ever, required to supply information on distractions that interfere with listening. We are, however, held accountable for the content of what is said, in spite of internal and/or external distractions which can destroy our listening effectiveness. Distractions, then, are a continuing problem that you face as a listener. But who is in the best position to overcome these interferences? You are, of course. If you are committed to the 51% minimum responsibility in communication, your effort to overcome distractions in listening is critical.

Dealing with Distractions

There are techniques you can use to combat internal and or external interferences. First, *identify the potential forces of distraction in all of your listening situations.* Second, *actively work* to reduce the distractions. To begin with, you need to look at your personal environment, and in particular at those conditions that relate to your listening activities. Make a list of the significant factors, especially those that are predictable. Start with your home life. List the people with whom you communicate and distractions that have interfered with communication in the past. Try to find ways to minimize or avoid the distractions in the future. Next, look at your work environment and finally, look at your social environment. Analysis should focus on location, time, people, subjects, and communication situations. Try to set aside time to think through these situations. Analysis on paper will advance your understanding immensely. Remember, to improve, you first need to identify where the problems are located (see Appendix C).

Whenever you have the opportunity to test and practice your ability to overcome listening distractions remember to: (1) prepare yourself to listen; (2) identify any distracting forces; (3) take steps to overcome or minimize the distractions; and (4) try to report the information later. To get information, you must first sense it and to make sure that you are sensing a message you must learn to overcome distractions that block your sensing. With all the pressures and demands of daily life, we normally find it difficult to overcome the myriad of distractions. As an example, Sara was busy working on her annual report when Dan came in to ask about plans for a technical writing seminar. At first Sara was listening, then she began to focus on her annual report and next the telephone rang. Luckily, at that moment, Sara realized that she was being distracted. Realizing her distraction she apologized to Dan, cleared her desk and asked her secretary to hold all calls until she and Dan were finished. Sara had regained control of the situation and was fully prepared to listen.

Some distractions occur spontaneously and can't be anticipated. In the same interaction, Dan mentioned Larry Nichols who was working on the project. The name Larry prompted thoughts of her husband Larry, whom she had just married, and momentarily she was off on a tangent. Again, Sara had to get back into the conversation with Dan. If her trip had been longer than a few seconds, it would have been best for Sara to ask Dan to repeat what was said so that nothing important would be missed (sensing).

Interruptions and distractions from our listening efforts are difficult to overcome because we are never sure exactly when they will occur. That's why you need to make a plan to reduce their likelihood of occurrence and to deal with them when they do arise. Internal distractions are the most difficult to control because they are triggered by factors such as external conditions, overloaded agendas, physical maladies, something a speaker says, or mental tangents. With such distractions, we are seldom forewarned and often fail to recognize them immediately. The key is to focus on the message content; look for value moments; plan to report; and develop a mental/summary of the message.

Overcoming Specific Distractions

You can overcome interferences by evaluating, anticipating, reviewing, and summarizing what the speaker is saying. Yet, any one of these techniques (evaluating, anticipating, reviewing or summarizing) can become a distraction in and of itself, and must be kept in bounds. You need to be careful, when asking yourself questions such as: How does this speaker know that? What evidence is being presented? What are the speaker's biases? If raised too frequently during a speech or conversation, such questions can become a distraction.

It is a difficult task, but you will profit if you evaluate, anticipate, review, and summarize while listening to messages. Using these techniques will help you to utilize the available time between your thought speed and the speaker's speech speed. Remember, wasting the thought speed–speech time differential can be dangerous because we are likely to go off on mental tangents.

The first step toward overcoming interferences is recognizing what your personal distractions are. See if you can separate your internal from your external interferences. Then, you can begin planning ways of mastering those interferences so that you will be in control of your own situation. (see Appendix C). As you read the next several examples, try to identify distractions that hinder you from listening to your best ability. Suggestions are given, but try to come up with your own personal strategy for helping to solve your listening distraction problems.

Clock-Watching

Many people are clock-watchers. As soon as we sit down to hear a lecture, sermon, report, or conversation, we automatically look at our watches. At times, of course, we may need to know the time because of scheduled appointments or a dinner date; however, many of us look at our watches for other reasons. Some people enter listening situations and then frequently check how much time they have before lunch, or position themselves in view of a clock so they can judge when a speaker will finish, and continue to keep a close eye on the time. As these people watch their watches and clocks, they fail to hear much of what is being said. If you're a clock-watcher and it interferes with your listening, what can you do about this distraction?

First, understand that your focus on time is itself a tremendous waste of time. Second, accept the minimum 51% responsibility challenge, and resolve to listen responsively. Third, plan to report to some specific person within 8 hours. Fourth, take purposeful notes, as appropriate. If you are involved in notetaking, you won't be as busy focusing on the time. Physically you have several other options. Stop wearing your watch, reverse it, or put it in your pocket or purse until after your meetings are over. It would also be a good idea not to sit where you could see a clock easily. You need to try to avoid temptations that function as distractions. The ultimate key is to remember the sage advice posted beneath many schoolroom clocks; "Time will pass! —— Will you?"

Telephones

Another distraction that many face at work and at home is the telephone. You may love to talk on the phone and appreciate its convenience, but telephones have the habit of ringing at times chosen by others. We have all found ourselves busy working on a project when we had to answer the phone. For this reason, we often miss vital information at the beginning of telephone conversations. Afterwards, we may wonder about the name of the person at the other end of the line, the name of their company, or what they wanted. In short, the telephone can serve as a distractor from our other listening situations, and of course we can be distracted while we listen on the telephone.

Where necessary, we should establish a system for dealing with the telephone in a manner that reduces its distractive impact. We seem to have a compulsion to get to the ringing phone. In fact, most of us will stop whatever we're doing to answer the phone. A personal review of options as to how a ringing phone should be handled can be profitable. Consider the use of answering machines, intermediaries (such as secretaries or assistants), transfer systems, and silencing switches.

We can also reduce our distractions when we are involved in telephone communication. Look at your office or home environment. Where is your phone located on your desk? Are you right-or left-handed? If your phone is on the right side of your desk and you are right-handed, then you probably pick up the phone with your right hand. If you do, you're distracted. As an alternative, place your phone on the left-hand side of your desk or answering space. Next, insure you have paper and pencil adjacent to every phone. Instead of picking up the phone when it first rings, always pick up your pencil first with your writing hand and get ready to listen. Now, as you answer the phone with your left hand, you have a pencil in hand and can write the vital information that comes at the beginning of the phone conversation. If you're left-handed, reverse the procedure.

Multiple Agendas

See if you can relate to the next interference problem: the multiple agenda. A woman makes plans to meet her husband for lunch. She wishes that she could have planned it for the next day since she has to pick up her airline ticket, meet with her accountant, and call on three customers. As this woman sits down to lunch with her husband, her multiple commitments—her internal interferences—begin working against her as a listener. She loves her husband and he said that their lunch date was important, but. . . . Before she realizes it, she is off on a mental tangent involving her multiple tasks. Not only will she not listen well, she also will not resolve her other obligations. She will lose on both ends. How can she overcome her distractions? First of all, she needs to prepare herself to listen, and plan to report what she's listening to right here. She must utilize the differential between her thought speed and speech speed to keep concentrating on the conversation she is involved in with her husband. Every time another agenda item enters her consciousness, she must make note to deal with it *later*. If they are seated, and the restaurant has a lot of external interferences such as noise from the kitchen, a disruptive party, or the cash register, she might be advised to ask for another table with fewer distractions.

Identify Interruptions

As we have seen, listening is interrupted in each of the above situations. When there is an interruption, it will have less of an effect if you have prepared yourself in advance (taken off your watch, moved your telephone, or chosen the best location to sit). To control the impact of interruptions, try to identify the interruption at the moment it occurs and say to yourself "Interruption! What did they just say? What are they saying? What are they going to say?" In this way you begin to acquire a reinforcement behavior to emphasize the importance of what was just said. Remember, the value lies in content!

Ask Questions

After identifying internal and external interruptions, you can also apply another technique to improve listening success: Ask questions. For example, when possible after you recognize that you have been interrupted, you should ask for the message to be repeated. As listeners, we need to understand that our task of reception as a listener is different from our task as a reader. In reading, you control the pace. In listening, the speaker controls the pace along with the environment, redundancy, repetition, and clarification. You can decide if you want to read this book in one day or read only a chapter now and continue later. If something is unclear you can look up a word in the dictionary or reread the passage to gain a better understanding of it. If you get tired of reading, you can take a nap; but what happens if you take a nap while listening? Often, you'll lose information. In some situations, if you're interrupted, the message flow stops while you deal with the interruption. In other cases, if you allow it, the message flow continues during the interruption. The aware, inquisitive listener can, at times, stop the flow temporarily.

Even though speakers control the flow of information, there are various ways in which you can affect the flow. At times, you can ask for repetition. In some situations, you can ask speakers to explain what they mean or ask the person to slow down. In many cases, we are captive listeners; yet, there are times when you can monitor what is being communicated by interjecting questions or comments.

If you are not in a position to ask what a word or phrase means, then you have to continue listening. If you don't, you will miss something else. There are times when you may not understand the vocabulary and professional jargon of speakers, and won't be able to ask a listener to explain. In these situations, you must control the distraction by not worrying about it. Make notes and strive for understanding with questions afterwards. Poor listeners get flustered when confronted with unfamiliar language or too much data and give up. To become good listeners, we need to learn to go beyond what we may have missed. It is better to lose one bit of information than to miss everything else while worrying about what you missed earlier.

LISTENING TO QUESTIONS

The suggestions presented in this chapter are designed to help you gain information more effectively when listening. Although most of our communication time is spent in receiving information, there are times such as when speaking to civic groups, press conferences, or board meetings when you are responsible for giving information to others. After these presentations, members of the audience often ask questions. If you have not prepared yourself to listen carefully, you may make mistakes which could affect your speaking success.

Before thinking about specific suggestions for ways to listen to questions, you should first think about why a person asks a question. Listeners ask questions for four basic reasons. They want: (1) to clarify points to improve their understanding; (2) to get more information or further support; (3) to satisfy their curiosity; or (4) to challenge the speaker. While listening, and before responding to a question, it helps to decide what the questioner's purpose or motive might be. Identifying a person's primary purpose for asking a question, enables you to answer the question with greater control and tact. Some speakers lose credibility by responding defensively when the questioner is not attacking them, but is merely confused or curious. Other speakers lose credibility by answering the wrong question or getting into side issues that are irrelevant.

The following guidelines should help you improve your question-answering ability.

1. *Listen carefully to the question*. Use all techniques appropriate to other listening situations.

2. If there is any confusion about what is being asked, paraphrase or repeat the question for the questioner.

3. Refer to the section of information that is pertinent to the question.

4. When clarification is necessary, explain the concept in different terms and provide different examples.

5. When further information is required, provide specific sources.

6. When a questioner challenges your position, provide further evidence to support your position.

7. Check back with the questioner to make sure that you answered the question satisfactorily.

SUMMARY

The effects of internal and external distractions combine in numerous ways to adversely influence our listening behavior. Distractions rob you of the ability to receive, process, and use information. Sensitivity in your personal listening habits is the first step toward improving listening. Second, try to think about the topic and situation in advance. Third, concentrate and try not to let your thoughts wander. Fourth, plan to report the general essence of what you are listening to to someone else.

With a positive listening attitude, it is easier to learn to ignore momentary distractions. To overcome recurring distractions, we must first identify interferences in our home, work, and social environments. Next, we need to actively work to reduce those distractions that hinder effective listening. Identifying and controlling distractions is a continuing challenge.

The next chapter discusses ways in which our emotions affect our listening behavior.

REFERENCES

Lefrancois, G. R. *Psychology*. Belmont, CA: Wadsworth, 1975.

Lorayne, H. *Remembering People: The Key to Success*. New York: Stein and Day, 1975.

Shiffrin, R. M., and Atkinson, R. C. Storage and retrieval processes in long-term memory. *Psychological Review*, 1969, **76**, 179.

7
Identifying and Dealing
with Emotions (A LOT)

*Congress is so strange. A man gets up to speak
and says nothing, nobody listens and then ev-
erybody disagrees.*

Will Rogers

In the last chapter we considered the effects of internal and
external distractions. This chapter focuses on an internal factor that is usually triggered by external stimuli—our emotions.

In listening, identification and control of our emotions is
one of the most important and most difficult skills to acquire. Emotional listeners have a tendency to be poor listeners because of their spontaneous reactions to people, topics
and language. To be able to control your emotions during
listening, you first need to develop methods of controlling
your emotions during communication. As we have noted,
you need to: (1) prepare and commit yourself to listen actively; (2) try to think about the topic and situation in advance;
(3) concentrate and try not to let your thoughts wander; (4)
look for useful material or information; (5) plan to report the
gist of what was said to someone else; and, (6) withhold
your judgment and reaction until you have fully received and
understood the speaker's position.

EMOTIONAL TRIGGERS

Poor listeners lose emotional control. Three areas wherein our emotions are affected during listening are: the speakers, the topics, and the words. Something about speakers, topics, and or language often triggers an emotional response that hinders the listening process. Try to think of a situation in which you lost your temper because of what someone said. Did you listen to anything after that? Probably not. Sometimes we also fail to listen to people just because of who they are. You may disagree with the political views of a well-known celebrity and immediately turn the channel to another station or you may fake attention to a supervisor with whom you just had an argument. These responses (signal reactions) are a function of listening habits and conditioning. When you lose emotional control, your filtering agents cause you to evaluate and respond prematurely. Subsequently, further sensing and interpreting of messages is also affected.

Four key points should give you a better understanding about the relationship between emotions and listening. First, *we all have emotional triggers*. All listening situations are affected by our emotions. Think about the last decision-making discussion you took part in. Did someone turn off or argue against something that they did not want to hear? On the other hand, we also have a tendency to not listen as carefully to topics with which we strongly agree. As your subjective and emotional reactions increase, your logical and rational abilities decrease. This is especially important in personal situations and is probably one reason that many doctors refrain from diagnosing or treating members of their immediate families. Their emotional involvement could affect their ability to make the best possible decisions in times of an emergency. In home, work and social situations, when emotionality goes up, rationality goes down.

The second key point to remember is that *our emotional reactions to speakers, topics and/or words are directly related to our filtering agents*. Just as the filter on a camera affects the final photograph, our past experiences, knowledge, beliefs, attitudes and opinions likewise affect our emotional responses. Our filtering agents are in a constant state of change and therefore we must continually work to identify and analyze our emotional triggers.

A third point to remember about emotional triggers is that *they affect our communication and listening effectiveness.* By referring to the SIER model (page 21), you can see that our emotional triggers primarily affect us at the evaluation level. When emotions or feelings are triggered, we make judgments which affect our responses. Emotional evaluations lead to emotional responses, but what makes the listening problem more difficult is that emotional evaluation also short-circuits our ability to listen at the lower but crucial levels of sensing and interpreting. If you tune out a speaker that advocates the passage of the Equal Rights Amendment, for example, then you cannot sense accurately, interpret correctly, make sound judgments or respond properly later to the complete message. Any response will be an emotional and usually inadequate one.

A fourth key point is that our *emotions may be triggered positively, neutrally, or negatively.* We usually don't think of positive emotions as causing listening problems, but if positive emotions are triggered, you tend to relax your listening effort. Since you like what you hear (or think you like what you hear), you may tend to relax and become passive. Consequently, you are susceptible to accepting half-truths, inconsistent data, opinions, etc. Often we agree and applaud before listening to the full message. However, just because of positive emotional responses, we shouldn't lose sight of our responsibility as listeners.

We usually link neutrality with objectivity, but a precaution needs to be given. When you are emotionally neutral, many listeners say "This doesn't matter to me," and tune out because of emotional disinterest. Allowing disinterest to control your behavior can lead to poor listening habits. On the other hand, emotional neutrality can lead to "objective" listening. Negative emotions trigger predictable behaviors. Such listeners usually stop listening, tune out, or become argumentative. If, for example, someone wants to cancel your favorite advertising campaign, if an automobile executive is required to attend a Ralph Nadar lecture, or if a speaker tells a joke about your ethnic origin, then you may have a tendency to respond emotionally. We quickly move to evaluation and response. Nevertheless, our goal is to never respond before we've fully comprehended, rationally interpreted, and appropriately evaluated a message.

A fifth key point, related to our pressing need to identify and control our emotional triggers, is that *this world is filled with individuals and organizations that are well trained, skilled, highly motivated, and well paid to discover the emotional triggers of others.*

Successful listeners know what causes them to respond emotionally and develop skill in controlling their emotional reactions. Your goal as an effective listener is to sense and interpret a message thoroughly and correctly, prior to your final evaluation and response.

WHO CONTROLS YOUR EMOTIONAL TRIGGERS?

How would you respond if you were asked, "Who controls your emotional triggers?" If typical, you would probably say "I do" or at least "I should." Yes, you should, but most people unconsciously allow others to play with their emotions. Without question, ineffective listeners don't control their listening emotionality. In fact, Hitler once said, "I know that one is able to win people far more by the spoken word, and that every great movement on this globe owes its rise to the great speakers and not to the great writers." Hitler and his associates were experts at controlling the emotional triggers of others. Currently, thousands of others throughout our universe are trained to control and manipulate our emotions. In all walks, advertising, education, politics, business, the clergy and the media, we see the skillful appeal to emotion.

While examining emotions that affect listening, there is one fact that we should keep in mind: You have emotional triggers and anyone who knows more about what triggers your emotions than you do is in a position to control you. Most important, we are not suggesting the elimination of our emotions. Even if we could, we shouldn't, as our emotions make us "alive"; however, in our quest for enhancing our listening skills, we need to recognize and control our emotional triggers, or others will. Think about it. You consume thousands of messages each day and behind those messages are people and organizations who are highly trained, skilled, motivated and financed to determine what affects your emotions. Millions of dollars worth of time and effort are spent to develop and send messages designed to trigger your emotions and reduce your ability to think rationally. Try to remind yourself as often as possible about the conscious effort given to messages designed to affect your emotional responses. Remember, *anyone who is in a position to know more about your emotional triggers than you do, is in a position to control you.*

The news headlines of the past few years provide numerous examples of such emotional influences. Were they rational when 913 people listened to the twisted Rev. James Jones's instructions to swallow the lethal grape drink at Jonestown? Were people responding logically when they stampeded supermarkets after Johnny Carson mentioned a rumor that there was a toilet paper shortage? Was Harry R. Truman logical when he refused to leave his home on the side of Mount St. Helens before it erupted? Were investors emotionally controlled when Joe Granville said "sell" and the market plummeted? Try to think of a time when you have spontaneously responded positively, neutrally, or negatively to a message and later wondered why? What triggered your response? If you want to be in control of your listening behavior, then you need to identify what affects your emotional triggers.

IDENTIFYING EMOTIONAL TRIGGERS

Let's begin by considering possible responses to situations in which others are involved. After examining these situations, we'll look at your own emotional responses.

1. Ronald Reagan discussing his proposal to eliminate federal loans for college students.

2. President of a major oil company proposing the deregulation of oil prices.

Identifying emotional triggers is an ongoing project that needs constant effort. You need to discover the *people, topics,* and *words* that influence your emotional responses. Remember, reading these examples can affect you positively, negatively or neutrally. In any communication situation, you need to first identify your emotional position and response tendencies. Let's start our analysis by looking at how certain people trigger our emotions.

People. We come in contact with all types of individuals each day. Without even realizing it, we respond to them. For practice, read the sample list of famous names. Beside the name, indicate how you would respond emotionally to each person by checking along the continuum.

	Positive	*Neutral*	*Negative*
1. Menachem Begin	_____	_____	_____
2. Johnny Carson	_____	_____	_____
3. Billie Jean King	_____	_____	_____
4. Mohammed Ali	_____	_____	_____
5. Jane Fonda	_____	_____	_____
6. Richard Nixon	_____	_____	_____
7. Jessie Jackson	_____	_____	_____
8. Jack Nicklaus	_____	_____	_____
9. Billy Graham	_____	_____	_____

	Positive	Neutral	Negative
10. Ronald Reagan	_____	_____	_____
11. A. Khomeini	_____	_____	_____
12. Mother Teresa	_____	_____	_____
13. Mike Wallace	_____	_____	_____
14. Reggie Jackson	_____	_____	_____
15. Ann Landers	_____	_____	_____

After completing the exercise, try to think of reasons for your responses. Our responses often prevent us from listening completely. These people are generally well known, but our emotional responses are not limited to famous people. Complete this analysis on your Target 25 list in the Personal Listening Profile (Chapter 4). Emotional response also occurs

Fig. 6.1 Visual Appearance Can Affect Listening

from visual stimuli. Look at the examples of clothing styles in Fig. 6.1 and again give your responses on the scale.

What characteristics of these clothing styles produced a response? Some of these outfits would be appropriate at home but not at work. Whenever we come in contact with others, we make judgments based on first impressions, but frequently these impressions are inaccurate. As you look at the people in your home, work, and social environments, try to think of the factors that influence you to respond positively, negatively, or neutrally. Try to minimize these factors that interrupt and distract your listening. Most important, analyze how your *emotional position* with respect to each person impacts on your listening to that person. How well do you listen to those to whose trigger you react positively? Neutrally? Negatively?

Identifying and analyzing people is an ongoing task. As our filtering agents change so do our emotional responses to people. It should be interesting to note where your emotional responses are consistent and inconsistent over a period of time. Right now, in fact, you can probably think of some people to whom you react differently today than you did a few months ago. On the other hand, our emotional response to certain others seems to never change. Keeping an updated notebook of how you are emotionally affected by the numerous people you listen to will yield significant benefits as you gain new insight into your own situation.

Topics

Now let's look at how you respond emotionally to selected topics. Below we have a sample list of items. Check your emotional responses as you did with the people exercises. As you do, think about the ways you listen when someone discusses these sample topics.

	Positive	*Neutral*	*Negative*
1. Gun control (Pro)	_____	_____	_____
2. Women in combat (Pro)	_____	_____	_____

	Positive	*Neutral*	*Negative*
3. Computerized dating (Pro)	_____	_____	_____
4. Equal rights Amendment (Neg)	_____	_____	_____
5. Space exploration (Pro)	_____	_____	_____
6. Capital punishment (Pro)	_____	_____	_____
7. Socialized medicine (Neg)	_____	_____	_____
8. Airline deregulation (Pro)	_____	_____	_____
9. Organized religion (Neg)	_____	_____	_____
10. Labor unions (Neg)	_____	_____	_____

For some, such topics tend to generate extreme emotional reactions. Think about what triggers your emotions with these topics. How about other topics? Identify other topics that affect your emotional triggers on the positive, neutral and negative scale. What affect do you note on your listening? Remember, the more diligent you are in your identification and analysis, the better you will be at controlling your emotions in listening situations.

Language

Some words cause immediate emotional responses. Buzzwords, labels, jargon, cliches, and profanity have a tendency to trigger our emotions. Again, to get you thinking about how words affect you emotionally, complete the following sample exercise by checking your emotional responses.

	Positive	Neutral	Negative
1. Republican			
2. Pig			
3. Jock			
4. Sex			
5. Intellectual			
6. Money saved is $ earned			
7. Honkie			
8. Bastard			
9. Strike			
10. Discrimination			
11. Democrat			
12. Kike			
13. Bitch			
14. Management			
15. Labor			

Think about how these words would affect you if used during a conversation or speech. You may feel that words don't strongly affect you, but they do. When we hear certain words during a conversation, we often evaluate and respond before we realize it.

Now that you have *started* a personal analysis of your emotional "hot spots," we need to observe that: (1) your success is directly related to your effort; (2) there are no right or wrong answers; and (3) your identification effort will work, but it should be a private task. (Be careful where you leave your notebooks, as you would any personal item.)

DEALING WITH EMOTIONS

Without question, emotions influence our ability to listen. The foregoing efforts toward identifying your emotional triggers is only a start. You now need to develop specific methods of *controlling* your emotions while listening. Emotional control is developed with *practice*. One of the best ways to practice is to consciously listen to the people, topics, and language that produce emotional responses and inhibit rationality. Again, you can use the SIER model as a guide. You first need to sense or hear what is being said and then fully understand what is meant. Then, and only then, are you in a position to effectively and rationally judge and respond to what has been said. A good method of learning control is to plan to report or make a commitment to report the essence of what you've heard to someone else.

Obviously it is difficult to conquer emotional responses with respect to people, topics, and language. It takes time and substantial effort. However, the following suggestions should help you. First, in every listening situation, identify prior to listening, those people, topics, and words that affect you emotionally. This practice will make you aware of the specific people, topics, and words that stimulate your reactions. Thus you are one step toward greater control. Next, attempt to analyze why these people, topics and words affect you the way they do. Think about your past experiences, or encounters that have influenced your emotional evaluation and reaction. Finally, try to reduce the impact of people, topics, and words on you by using a "defense" mechanism. One which is popularly suggested to help avoid emotional reactions is called "rationalization." Rationalization involves attempting to convince yourself that the person, topic, or word is not as bad or good as you think. No matter what defense mechanism you use, try to eliminate your emotionally conditioned response to people, topics, or words. Three additional suggestions which should help you compensate for an initial bias (positive or negative) are: (1) *Defer judgment.* As we have mentioned, you need to listen to an entire message before responding. (2) *Empathize.* Try to take the speaker's point of view while you listen. Search for reasons for the speaker's views and arguments, even if they are different from your own. (3) *Place your personal feelings in perspective.* Remember that your past experiences, including your cultural and educational background, have molded you into a unique person. If you critically evaluate your own views, then you should be better able to relate to the ideas of others.

The suggestions that have been presented throughout this chapter should help your emotional control during listening, but for the techniques to be useful, you must incorporate and practice them. You've first got to know what triggers your emotions and then you have to develop control through practice.

SUMMARY

Controlling emotional response is one of the most important and difficult listening skills to develop. Any aspect associated with people, topics, or language may trigger or encourage emotional reactions while listening. Five key points help explain the relationship between emotions and listening. (1) All people have emotional triggers. (2) Emotions are directly related to filtering agents. (3) Emotional triggers affect communication and listening effectiveness. (4) Emotions may be affected positively, negatively, and or neutrally. (5) Some professionals are trained to understand what affects emotional responses in others. For this reason it is important to know what influences our emotions. Anyone who is in a position to know more about what triggers your emotions than you do is in a position to control you. It is possible to deal with emotions if they are identified prior to listening, if there is an attempt to analyze what people, topics, and language affect emotions and if attempts are made to reduce the impact of aroused emotions. Such control must be practiced and incorporated into everyday listening situations to be effective. The next chapter deals with messages; we will consider methods for identifying message structures, explaining how to evaluate and respond to messages, and discuss techniques of notetaking.

8

Identifying Message Structures and Notetaking

The reason you don't understand me, Edith, is because I'm talking to you in English and you're listening in dingbat!

Archie Bunker

The last two chapters offered suggestions to help identify distractions and emotional triggers that hinder your listening effectiveness. By keeping these principles in mind, you should be able to control your internal and external interferences and emotional responses to people, topics, and language. This chapter should help you receive and remember more of the oral messages you hear by explaining how to identify message structures and providing directions for taking better, more productive, notes.

IDENTIFYING MESSAGE STRUCTURES: UNIVERSAL PROBLEMS

As listeners, we face three universal problems: (1) we listen faster than average speakers speak; (2) we often fail to use the thought/speech–speed time differential productively; and

(3) we usually do not take effective mental and/or written notes. Poor listeners generally have difficulty in all three of these areas. Fortunately, you may have already begun to deal with the first two problems after reading and doing the exercises in earlier chapters. One way to approach the third problem is by learning to listen for organizational arrangement patterns that speakers use. The following list emphasizes, once again, differences between poor and good listeners that relate to message structure. Poor listeners do not:

1. Plan to report what they hear later to someone else.

2. Use the thought/speech speed differential to their advantage.

3. First look for the central idea and organizational pattern.

4. Take mental or written notes.

5. Adapt their listening to the organizational pattern of the speaker.

6. Anticipate the organizational pattern of the speaker.

7. Control diversion onto mental tangents that waste listening time.

Good listeners do:

1. Plan to report what they hear later.

2. Use the thought/speech speed differential to their advantage.

3. First look for the central idea and organizational pattern.

4. Take mental and/or written notes.

5. Adapt their listening to the organizational pattern of the speaker.

6. Anticipate the organizational pattern of the speaker.

7. Not waste time on mental tangents.

As listeners, we have to learn to adapt to a speaker's organization. A speaker's presentation is ordinarily somewhere between being carefully organized and completely disorganized. Whether a speaker's primary purpose is, phatic (small-talk binding), catharsis (venting), information, or persuasion; whether the situation is formal or informal; whether the speaker is prepared or unprepared; or whether the oral message is presented one to one or one to many, speakers fall on an organizational continuum. Try if you will to recall the last speaker you heard. You may have heard the president's "state of the union address," a sermon, a seminar lecture, a telephone chat, a community service meeting, or discussion around the fire. What do you remember about the speaker's message? Using this organizational continuum, where would you place the speaker?

Very				Very
Organized				Unorganized
	Moderately		Moderately	
	Organized	N	Unorganized	

Why? You may not remember anything about the speaker's organization. If you don't, you need to start a plan for remembering the speaker's organizational habits and behaviors in order to make them work for you. You can get the speaker to work for you by first identifying whether or not the speaker is organized. If the speaker is organized, you need to find out how, and then adjust your listening to that structure. If the speaker is not organized, you need to find a method of organizing the unorganized message.

The key is to identify and adapt your listening to a speaker's organizational pattern. This is one way of using the advantage of your thought speed which is faster than the speaker's speech speed. Later in this chapter, typical organizational patterns will be explained. If you can tune in to the speaker's organizational pattern, you will have a clearer picture of the entire message. By seeing a message structure, you have a skeleton framework for the message. This skeleton gives you a pattern with which to attach the supporting data which helps you remember the message. Even with disorganized speakers, using a pattern will help you make sense out of a speaker's disorganized confusion. One final note: most speakers are habitual, and thus predictable, in the degree and nature of organizing material they use. By listening to "cue" and "clue" language you can determine if and how speakers are structured.

MESSAGE STRUCTURES

The first step toward identifying an organizational pattern is to see if there is a message structure. Speakers can be seen to organize their ideas either climactically or anticlimactically. A climactic structure builds to a final conclusion. Mystery writers characteristically build their plots climactically. Readers are never sure of "who done it" until the final page of the book. In an anticlimactic structure, the conclusion is known from the beginning of the message.

Speakers who arrange their material by giving general information first and work to more specific information later use climactic structures. One example of a climactic presentation would be:

> *It's a pleasure to warn you*
> *Of the thief of life.*
> *This thief shortens your breath!*
> *This thief befouls your nest!*
> *This thief diminishes your savings!*
> *This thief reduces your friends!*
> *This thief ruins your clothing!*
> *This thief blackens your lungs!*
> *This thief steals your life!*
> *Smoking is a thief of life.*

From this example, you see that the speaker was well organized. The speaker moved from general information to specific conclusions. You may not agree with the speaker's conclusion, but this type of organizational structure usually gets attention. Listeners stay tuned in until the end so that they can find out "what happens." Effective listeners would recognize this climactical pattern immediately and listen to the detailed information because it supports the conclusion drawn in the end. If you fail to listen well to the details, it is impossible for you to adequately understand and evaluate what you've heard. In other words, you stand the chance of making interpretive, evaluative, and responding errors.

The same message could also be developed anticlimactically. The speaker's organization moves from a specific idea to a general conclusion. For example:

Smoking is a thief of life.
Smoking is harmful to your health,
Your finances, your personal
Relationships, and your longevity!
Smoking is indeed a thief and I've got proof!

Smoking shortens your breath!
Smoking befouls your nest!
Smoking costs you money!
It ruins your clothing!
It costs you friends!
It blackens your lungs!
It steals your life!

An anticlimactic organizational structure can affect the quality of your listening in several ways. If you agree (positive trigger) with the issue, then you might relax your listening and miss a point. In contrast, if you disagree (negative trigger), you may critically build a refutation and again miss something important. We see that one disadvantage of the anticlimactic organizational structure is that it does not serve to hold attention like a climactic structure does. Be sure as you identify these structures that you continue to listen by planning to report what you've heard to someone else afterwards. Again, if you practice withholding judgments, listening to the entire message, and plan to report later, you will listen better and retain more. Your notetaking should be adapted to the speaker's structure or organizational pattern, which we discuss next.

ORGANIZATIONAL PATTERNS

There are numerous organizational patterns available to speakers. These patterns are used in combination with the climactic and anticlimactic structures. We'll look at four of the most typical organizational patterns: enumeration, problem/solution, time-sequence (chronological), and spatial. There are of course others, as you will discover.

The first of these common patterns is *enumeration*. As the word suggests, speakers organize their message around a given number of points. You have heard speakers use this pattern on numerous occasions: "My first four points are . . .", "The topic can be divided into three areas", or "There are six steps you should follow." Following is a more detailed example:

> I'm happy that you could join me this morning to discuss our fund-raising campaign. There are four points we need to cover.
>
> *First*, is setting our goal. We need to establish a realistic figure and subdivide it into targets for each department.
>
> *Second*, we need to identify our potential population.
>
> *Third*, outline our strategy.
>
> *Fourth*, setting completion dates for each strategy.

The enumeration pattern is extremely clear, since the speaker's cue language is direct; if you adapt to the speaker's structure, you should end up remembering substantially more information. (Even though enumeration is easy to follow, you will find that there are some drawbacks.) Speakers tend to use enumeration when they want to explain. Pure explanation can be boring when there is too much information to remember. If you find a speaker outlining more than three or four main points, try to take notes. Picking out the main points numerically should help you take better notes and thus retain more.

Another commonly used organizational pattern is the *problem/solution* pattern. When using this pattern, speakers usually focus on either the nature of the problem, its causes, effects, and solutions, or a combination of the four components. The following examples will help to illustrate.

> Ladies and gentlemen, we face a grievous *problem. We are the only major city in the entire state that does not have fluoridated water.* And this problem has been recognized by the dental association. . . .

Or the speaker may primarily develop the *cause* of a problem:

> Ladies and gentlemen, for months we have recognized the problem of our nonfluoridated water supply. Tonight I want to discuss the *cause* of our problem. As you well know, *our city engineer and city council have taken the position that.* . . .

Or the speaker may primarily develop the *effect* of a problem:

> Ladies and gentlemen, we must examine the *effect* of this fluoridation problem on our youthful population. The *primary effect of our nonfluoridated water will show up in our children's teeth. The effect will be increased cavities, increased dental bills, increased.* . . .

Or the speaker may primarily develop the *solution* of a problem:

> Ladies and gentlemen, the *solution* is complex but necessary. If we are to reduce this problem, we *must obtain the support of the majority of this community*—the solution will require . . . .

As we listen, we should be able to ascertain whether or not the speaker is zeroing in on the problem, its causes, effects, or solution, or a combination (i.e., problem and cause, or problem and solution). When trying to identify the organization pattern, the key is to listen to the speaker's "cue" language. After you have identified the speaker's central purpose and developed a structural skeleton, and adapted your notetaking (mental or written) to this structure, you will find yourself remembering more of the total message.

Using a *time-sequence* or chronological pattern is a third scheme of message organization. A speaker can trace a topic by looking at the past and building to the present and or future, or by looking at the present and digressing through the past. This pattern helps listeners with recall by pointing out relationships through the chronological progressions. Consider this example:

> If we analyze the widespread use of drugs in our society, we see a clear-cut *change over the years. Historically,* we can track the relative non-use by young persons of any drugs in the United States *up to the mid-1960's.* Without question, the widespread use of illegal drugs was nonexistent until the "beat generation" of the *1950's and 60's.* But the generation gap: the Vietnam War, the social revolution, and the political reaction of the mid-*1960's* corresponds with the growth and widespread use of numerous drugs, and this growth continued into the mid-*1970's.* However, by the latter part of the 1970's, we can see an interesting trend. In this time period, a general decline in the widespread use of illegal drugs is noted.
>
> And as we *look to the future* experts are predicting further change. . . .

In this situation, the speaker develops the message around a clear-cut time sequence pattern. Again, cue words that speakers use will help you identify the chronological pattern: "Let's look back to our beginnings . . .", or "An analysis of the past twelve years should show. . . ." Your listening will improve as you learn to adjust to a speaker's organizational pattern.

The fourth pattern that we will discuss is the *spatial, graphic,* or *pictorial technique.* This device is an interesting one for listeners because the speaker typically draws a picture to help explain the points being made. By tuning in to the speaker's cue language you will be able to determine whether or not the spatial pattern is being used. Take the following example:

> I heard an interesting speaker at our professional meeting today. Mr. Strand, a renowned financial investment expert, was explaining what it took to be financially successful in this country today. He suggested that we *needed to picture in our minds eye, the ladder of financial success.* He said that we have to climb four rungs on this ladder if we want to be financially successful. The first rung he talked about was a solid, thorough, liberal education. He said education was critical because. . . . The second rung he talked about was our contacts. He said the family we were born into, the people we went to school with, the people we worked with, lived with, and socialized with, all had an important impact on our financial success. The third rung he talked about was our long-term motivation. He said that every study of financially successful people showed high motivation. And finally, the fourth rung on his ladder of success was the most important of all. And you know as long as I saw that picture of his ladder of success with its four rungs, I can easily remember his key points. I carried more information out of that presentation than any I can remember for a long time.

This speaker used graphic examples to add emphasis to the presentation. If you begin to picture what the speaker is describing in your mind's eye, you will get more of the message. By also drawing upon your visual senses, you will perceive the organizational skeleton more readily. Remember, the speaker's cue words and language will help show which pattern is being used. Finally, your notes should reflect the graphic structure.

Speakers often use these four patterns in combination, or they may use altogether different patterns. The key for listeners is to pick out one arrangement as the primary pattern and another as a secondary pattern where evident. Using these patterns of arrangement will help you overcome the problems of wasting the speech–thought differential, poor notetaking, and listening primarily for facts rather than concepts. If the speaker is organized, listen for the central ideas and try to develop a skeleton to attach the facts. Use the speaker's structural system. If the speaker is unorganized, you need to recognize the lack of organization. Next you need to use any one of the four arrangement patterns to organize the material for your own use. Effective listeners have their favorite organization systems that they can quickly turn to when needed. These patterns have been used in the past to help speakers; you can use the same principles to help improve your ability to listen.

SOME HINTS FOR NOTETAKING

Closely related to the listening process is the process of taking notes. You have frequently employed notetaking in classroom situations or meetings, but it is also appropriate in other public speaking or semiformal listening situations. Below are several suggestions designed to help you improve your notetaking ability (Barker, 1971).

(1) *Decide whether or not to take notes.* Notes may be useful in some settings, but unnecessary, and even distracting in others. Your purpose for listening should determine whether or not you need to take notes. If you feel you may need to refer to the information at a future time, the notes probably are necessary. However, if the information is for immediate use (e.g., announcements about the day's schedule at a summer workshop), it may be more effective simply to listen carefully without taking notes. Your own ability to comprehend and retain information is a variable which also must be taken into account. If you have high concentration and retention

abilities, you probably will need to take relatively few notes. However, if you have difficulty remembering information the day after it is presented, you probably should get out a notepad.

(2) *Decide what types of notes are necessary.* There are at least three different types of notes which people may elect to take. They differ in purpose and specificity. These three common types are key words, partial outline, and complete outline.

   (a) *Key words.* When you primarily want to remember some specific points in the message, key word notes are probably the most efficient. For example, if you wanted to remember an entertaining story about a member of the Democratic party who attended a meeting of the John Birch Society by mistake, so you could retell it later, you might elect to write the key words, "DP at Birch meeting," on your notepad. Key words are used to help provide cues for ideas which were presented during the listening setting. However, unless you can positively associate the meaning with the key words, they are not useful.

   (b) *Partial outline.* If you decide that there are several important elements you should remember in a message, it probably is desirable to take notes in partial outline form. The points in the message which seem important to you are noted rather completely, and other points which you do not deem important are not recorded. For example, suppose you are auditing a night class on statistics; your professor illustrates how to compute a mean, median, and mode, but you may decide that you want to remember only how to compute the mode. Consequently, you record in your notes only that portion of the lecture that relates to your specific interest. The notes you take are complete, but they do not represent all of the material that was presented.

(c) *Complete outline*. In many listening situations, it is important to record most of what is presented. In meetings and in other settings where you may need to have a complete record of what was said, a complete set of notes in outline form is necessary, because you often will be expected to provide specific information at a later time. Of course, the outline form should be adapted to the speaker's format.

The key is to determine in advance what type of notes you will need to take in a given listening setting, and then adapt your notetaking accordingly. If you modify your notetaking according to the demands of the situation and the speaker's system, you will make most efficient and effective use of your efforts.

(3) *Keep notes clear.* This involves not only using brief sentences and statements of ideas which are understandable after you have written them, but also includes such details as not cluttering the page, not scribbling, and not writing side comments. Use the paper efficiently; avoid crowding words together.

(4) *Keep notes brief.* This suggestion speaks for itself. The briefer your notes, the less time you will be spending writing, and the less likely you will be to miss what the speaker says.

(5) *Recognize as quickly as possible the organizational pattern (or lack of pattern) of the speaker.* First, as mentioned earlier, be aware of the fact that many speakers have no discernible orgainzational pattern. There is a tendency for some notetakers to try to organize notes on the basis of their own preferred patterns rather than the speaker's. For example, you may normally outline beginning with roman numeral I, followed by A and B, 1 and 2, a and b, and so forth. However, if the speaker is simply talking in random fashion without much formal organization, then artificially imposing an organizational pat-

tern on the message may distort its meaning. Therefore, it is important to determine quickly if the speaker is employing a formal organizational pattern and adapt your own notetaking to this pattern.

(6) _Review your notes soon afterwards._ This suggestion is extremely important in a learning situation because by reviewing information frequently we retain it longer. Ideas that we hear once tend to be forgotten within 24 hours. Without some review they may be lost to us forever. Another reason for reviewing your notes soon after taking them is that you may remember some details at that point which you might not remember when reading your notes at some future time.

SUMMARY

Messages range on a continuum from very unorganized to very well organized and we need to adapt our listening to a speaker's pattern. This chapter described how message structures are organized either climactically or anticlimactically. There are numerous organizational patterns available to speakers. The four used most often are: enumeration, problem/solution, time-sequence (chronological), and spatial. Several hints for notetaking were given. Listeners should: (1) Decide whether or not to take notes; (2) Decide what type of notes are necessary; (3) Keep notes clear; (4) Keep notes brief; (5) Find the organizational pattern (or recognize the lack of pattern) as quickly as possible; and (6) Review the notes later. The next chapter suggests techniques for message evaluation and response.

REFERENCE

Barker, L.L. _Listening Behavior._ Englewood Cliffs, NJ: Prentice-Hall, 1971.

9

Message Evaluation and Response

The greatest compliment that was ever paid me was when one asked me what I thought, and attended to my answer.

Henry David Thoreau

Overcoming distractions and emotions enables you to sense and interpret messages more accurately, but your ultimate listening goal is to make appropriate evaluations and responses. The skilled listener is an evaluating and responsive listener. Successful listening requires accurate evaluations and judgments about what you have heard and understood. You cannot effectively evaluate what you do not completely sense or properly interpret. On the other hand, even messages that you sense and interpret accurately can nevertheless be misevaluated, as we shall explain.

TYPES OF EVALUATION

Message evaluation is either immediate or delayed. Immediate evaluation is appropriate when messages are short, noncontroversial, or uncomplicated. Delayed evaluation is best for long, controversial, or complex messages. When a fellow employee asks if you'd like to go on a coffee break it's easy for you to make a decision without too much thought, but if the same employee asked you if some planned price increases would be sufficient to meet rising costs, you would probably need time to look at all the issues involved before answering.

As listeners we need to guard against premature evaluation, especially for complex issues. Premature evaluations are caused by uncontrolled emotional responses. Evaluation should take place only after you have considered whether or not the message is factual or opinionated, the content development is sound, the evidence supports the message, and the reasoning based on the evidence is valid. If one of your friends were to encourage you to buy a house in his or her neighborhood, you would expect your friend's viewpoint to be somewhat biased. Your friend would even have a stronger bias if he or she were also a real estate broker.

It is a good idea when listening for you to keep in mind whether or not the information is based on fact or opinion. Obviously, a friend who lives in the neighborhood is probably pleased with the school system, road maintenance, and neighbors, but he or she may subconsciously fail to mention some factors that are undesirable (floods during the spring, or no dog leash laws). This is not to say that decisions should not be based on opinion. We accept opinions daily; yet, in subsequent evaluation, we should attempt to determine the degree of objectivity a person has.

After a speaker makes a statement you need to look at the content. If a real estate broker were to tell you that the neighborhood is crime-free, the house is energy-efficient, and there is an assumable mortgage, you might be ready to buy. However, you need to stop and think about what you may not have been told. Is the house near a railroad track, is the basement waterproof, or are there problems with appliances? We need to listen for details of the total picture before responding and making a decision. Important information may be missing even though you have heard and understood everything that has been said.

Next in evaluating the content of the message, you need to weigh how the information was supported. Did your friend's opinions come from others in the area, statistics from local newspapers on housing costs, or facts from meter readings? For example, if you are told that a house is energy-efficient, you need to know who says so and how do they know. Did the information come from the previous owner, the contractor, or someone else? Is the information from recent reports or was it given several years ago? It could make a big difference in the cost of heating oil if costs were from 1975 instead of today.

Finally, after determining whether the information is based on fact or opinion, and after evaluating the content and evidence used, you need to look at the speaker's reasoning. You want to know if the conclusions reached by the speaker are logical, and based on the evidence given. If your friend says that the house is in a good location because the windows are shaded in the summer and hit by the sun in the winter, then that should help to cut energy costs. However, if your friend were to say that the shade trees help keep energy costs low but they do not shade the house's windows in the summer or let sunlight in during the winter, the reasoning would be questionable. It is important to remember to evaluate all sides when listening to messages. If you do you will be in a better position when making your decisions.

So far we have stressed the importance of waiting to hear the complete message before evaluating it. Along with avoiding premature evaluation, you also need to learn to identify biased communication. Two types of biased communication that listeners should be especially aware of are rumors and propaganda.

Rumors

Rumors may or may not be started deliberately, whereas propaganda is carefully developed. Of course, all communication is biased to a certain extent. Examples of rumors are numerous. If you think about your interpersonal communication activities during the past week, it is likely that you can remember several rumors which you either heard or were instrumental in sending to others. Rumors range from personal rumors about yourself or your friends to large-scale rumors about governmental policy and international affairs.

Rumors have characteristics that can help you identify them: (1) Rumors are usually temporary in nature; (2) Rumors tend to run in cycles; (3) The content of most rumors deals with people or events; (4) Verification of a rumor is usually difficult or impossible; (5) Initiators of rumors generally are not experts regarding the subject of the rumor. Because few people are experts on a variety of different subjects, the possibility of rumor is high. People are often so busy that they do not have or want to take the time to verify rumors which therefore tend to escalate. A few years ago, it was rumored that a major fast food chain was using red worms to increase the protein rate in their hamburgers. This rumor ended up costing the company millions of dollars, since the chain had to develop an extensive advertising campaign to refute and reassure their customers.

There are several things listeners can do to avoid being deceived or misinformed by rumors. First, you must identify a message as a rumor. Five checks will help you determine whether or not the information is valid.

1. Check the source.

2. Check with the sender of the rumor to determine the basis of the information contained in the rumor.

3. Determine the consequences of the rumor for you and other people concerned.

4. Try to assess what motives might have contributed to the rumor.

5. Attempt to investigate systematically to uncover evidence which will prove or disprove the critical elements of the rumor.

The suggestions listed above are also useful in assessing propaganda. The following section describes the nature of propaganda and gives several additional suggestions to help us identify and deal with propaganda.

Propaganda

If you can't do anything to improve on the silence, don't disturb it.

Anonymous

Most people associate negative connotations with the term propaganda. Propaganda is usually thought of in connection with subversive elements in society such as communists, "moonies," or fascists. However, common connotation is often misleading. In fact, propaganda exists in most newspapers and magazines that you read every day. There is nothing inherently bad about propaganda. It is simply a form of communication with built-in biases. Propaganda involves a conscious attempt to influence others. Its purpose may be either good or bad. Propaganda that attacks unequal employment opportunities, disease, monopolies, organized crime, or governmental bureaucracy is generally considered desirable. The desirability is not reduced because the appeals are primarily emotional rather than intellectual. In fact, most messages that use excessively emotional appeals are a form of propaganda. Propaganda exists in all communication media and we need to be able to recognize and analyze these types of biased messages.

One characteristic of propaganda campaigns is an increase in the number and intensity of rumors circulated. Rumors and propaganda are interrelated because rumors and propaganda thrive on each other. When examining the purpose of a message, the most important test is to determine whether the communicator or the general public will benefit from the ideas presented. If the suggested plan benefits the originators of the message and their interests primarily, the message may be seen as propaganda. Keep in mind that the fact that a message does happen to be biased does not necessarily mean that the results would be bad. Propaganda may benefit the originator as well as members of society. For example, with increasing crime rates numerous security systems have been marketed using emotional appeals. Yet, buying a security system for your home is beneficial to you and the promoter.

Following are some of the devices or signals which help us to identify propaganda in messages. *Half truths* involve telling only part of the story deliberately when the full story is known. *Card stacking* is a type of lie presenting only one side of an argument, and withholding information which might refute the position being advocated. *Hasty generalization* refers to distorting or carelessly misquoting the findings of a study or misrepresenting the findings by generalizing to a larger population than is justifiable. *Name-calling* is a device used to attack or degrade the personality of an opponent or opposing group. *Plain folks* devices attempt to make the speaker appear humble and one of the crowd by using such things as middle-or lower-class language, dressing conservatively or specifically for the situation. Finally, the *bandwagon* device is employed to show that "everyone else is doing it." These are only some of the devices used, but now we need to identify some methods of analysis.

Propaganda assessment is more difficult than rumor analysis because the source of the message is often unknown, and the full evidence is usually not available for examination. However, in trying to determine whether the message is a form of propaganda, first you need to carefully analyze what is being said. Then you should look at the evidence and try to determine who will benefit most from what is suggested. Again remember to use these principles along with the suggestions for analyzing rumors. The importance of active critical listening in the analysis of rumors and propaganda cannot be overemphasized. As a critical listener you can help repress unfounded rumors and minimize the negative effects of propaganda on yourself and others.

MESSAGE RESPONSE (FEEDBACK)

The spoken word belongs half to him who
speaks, and half to him who hears.

French Proverb

As a listener, one of your final tasks is to develop the ability to respond appropriately to messages. Until a listener responds, there is no way to know if he or she has sensed, interpreted and evaluated the message fully and effectively. A necessary element of the completed communication process is feedback or response. A successful listener will not neglect the responsibility to respond. As mentioned earlier, feedback helps speakers to know if they have been understood, and if they are interesting, etc. Feedback also helps you personally. The feedback you receive when you listen to yourself can help you correct mistakes in the future. For example, if you mispronounce a person's name, it is important to hear that so you will pronounce it correctly later. Responding to communication helps you to control some aspects of your own and other speakers' behavior.

Earlier, we explained the differences between positive, negative, and ambiguous feedback. There are also four classes of feedback response: verbal feedback, nonverbal feedback, combined verbal and nonverbal feedback, and the absence of verbal and nonverbal feedback (silence). Think of all the times you have sent feedback verbally today. You probably answered questions and also gave spontaneous remarks such as commenting on someone's clothing, absence, or punctuality. Nonverbal feedback is sent continually. Nonverbal feedback takes the form of body motions or vocal intonations and provides a significant amount of information in face-to-face interactions. Listeners usually respond verbally and nonverbally to messages. We tend to respond verbally and nonverbally without thinking about it. Think about a time when you gave directions to someone. It was probably natural for you to explain verbally while using your arms and hands to point and indicate directions. The last class of feedback is silence. We often neglect silence as a pattern of responding to messages. We are all familiar with the "silent treatment," yet silence can also be used positively to communicate concentration or sympathy.

We use feedback for different purposes. Feedback can be rewarding or punishing. Perceptions of reward and punishment differ from person to person. What is rewarding to one person may be punishing to another. For example, some employees accept negative criticism positively as a method to improve, but others feel as though they are being attacked. Another purpose of feedback that managers use very often is nondirective or directive feedback. Nondirective feedback is an attempt to replicate what has been said in an effort to encourage further discussion. Directive feedback places a value judgment on what has been said and is concerned with reward and punishment. Managers listen to employees explain why a project is delayed, giving nondirective feedback. After the employee's explanation the manager often responds with directive feedback about what should be done in the future. Effective listeners don't rely on one purpose for giving feedback, but try to adjust their feedback to meet the demands of the situation.

As listeners we are concerned with communicating our responses accurately to others. Listeners have the duty to respond to a message in order to complete the communication process. The following guidelines should help you increase your feedback effectiveness.

1. Send feedback that is appropriate to the speaker, message, and context.

2. Send the feedback promptly.

3. Make certain the feedback is clear in meaning.

4. Be certain the speaker perceived the feedback.

5. Beware of overloading the system.

6. Delay in performing any activity that might create an unintentional effect.

7. Keep feedback to the message separate from personal evaluation.

8. Use nondirective feedback until the speaker invites evaluation of the message.

9. Be sure that you understand the message before you send directive feedback.

10. Realize that early attempts at giving more effective feedback may seem unnatural but will improve with practice.

SUMMARY

Total listening involves evaluation and response. In this chapter we discussed differences between immediate and delayed evaluation. Evaluation should take place only after you have considered whether or not the message content is factual or opinionated, the reasoning is sound, and the evidence is timely, supportive, and valid. We considered the characteristics of rumor and propaganda, and finally, the types of response or feedback were discussed.

Epilogue

It seems that we shall eventually come to believe that the responsibility for effective oral communication must be equally shared by speakers and listeners. When this transpires, we shall have taken a long stride toward greater economy in learning, accelerated personal growth, and significantly deepened human understanding.

Ralph C. Nichols and Leonard A. Stevens *Are You Listening?*
(McGraw Hill, 1957, p. 221-22)

Appendix A

The exercises in this appendix are designed to help you extend your understanding of the various communication purposes and stages. Specifically, you will have an opportunity to analyze your communication relationships and practices—past, present, and future. Exercise 1 focuses on identifying "primary" and "secondary" communicators with whom you relate. Exercise 2 examines the nature of your "phatic," "cathartic," "informational," and "persuasive" communication. Exercise 3 will help you utilize the SIER formula to understand and maximize your listening practices.

EXERCISE 1

Periodically identify (by name) your communication connections. Who do you spend measurable time listening to?

Primary Communicators: List by name individuals with whom you communicate regularly (i.e., everyday or several times a day).

Name   Relationship

_____   _____

_____   _____

_____   _____

_____   _____

_____   _____

_____   _____

_____   _____

_____   _____

_____   _____

_____   _____

_____   _____

_____   _____

_____   _____

_____   _____

Secondary Communicators: List by name individuals with whom you communicate periodically (i.e., a few times per week).

Name   Relationship

_____   _____

_____   _____

_____   _____

_____   _____
_____   _____
_____   _____
_____   _____
_____   _____
_____   _____
_____   _____
_____   _____
_____   _____
_____   _____
_____   _____
_____   _____

EXERCISE 2

Analyze *why* (purposes) and *how well* you communicate with specific individuals and how you can *improve*.

• Phatic (Binding) Communication

Name ten individuals with whom you experience productive phatic communication:

Name	Relationship	Why
_____	_____	_____
_____	_____	_____
_____	_____	_____
_____	_____	_____

_____	_____	_____
_____	_____	_____
_____	_____	_____
_____	_____	_____
_____	_____	_____
_____	_____	_____

In the "Why" column, briefly, indicate why you believe you experience productive phatic communication with each of the foregoing individuals.

Name ten individuals with whom you should, but *do not* experience productive phatic communication.

Name	Relationship	Why Not
_____	_____	_____
_____	_____	_____
_____	_____	_____
_____	_____	_____
_____	_____	_____
_____	_____	_____
_____	_____	_____
_____	_____	_____
_____	_____	_____
_____	_____	_____

In the "Why Not" column, briefly identify why you believe you do not experience productive phatic communication with each of the foregoing individuals.

In each case, what can you *do* specifically to improve the existing or desired phatic communication?

• Cathartic (Venting) Communication

Name ten individuals who serve your cathartic needs.

Name	Relationship
_____	_____
_____	_____
_____	_____
_____	_____
_____	_____
_____	_____
_____	_____
_____	_____
_____	_____
_____	_____

Generally speaking, how important is their listening to your catharsis and what are their observable characteristics?

Name ten individuals who should, but *do not* serve your cathartic needs.

Name	Relationship
_____	_____
_____	_____
_____	_____
_____	_____
_____	_____
_____	_____
_____	_____

_____   _____
_____   _____
_____   _____

In your opinion, why do these individuals not serve your cathartic needs? What are their observable characteristics? What is the impact of this cathartic neglect?

Name ten individuals whose cathartic communication needs *you serve* as a listener.

Name	Relationship
_____	_____
_____	_____
_____	_____
_____	_____
_____	_____
_____	_____
_____	_____
_____	_____
_____	_____
_____	_____

Why?

What is the impact?

Name ten individuals whom *you can serve better* as a cathartic listener.

<u>Name</u>   <u>Relationship</u>

_____   _____

_____   _____

_____   _____

_____   _____

_____   _____

_____   _____

_____   _____

_____   _____

_____   _____

_____   _____

How? Outline your strategy on paper.

• Informational Communication

Name ten key individuals whom you communicate with for informational purposes.

<u>Name</u>   <u>Relationship</u>

_____   _____

_____   _____

_____   _____

_____   _____

_____   _____

_____   _____

_____   _____

---   ---
---   ---
---   ---

Outline three ways that your informational listening could be improved with each individual.

Name ten individuals that you should, but *do not*, communicate with well for informational purposes.

Name	Relationship

Why not?

Specifically, what can you do to enhance your listening for information with each individual?

• Persuasive Communication

Name ten key individuals that you communicate with well for purposes of persuasion.

<u>Name</u>   <u>Relationship</u>

_____   _____

_____   _____

_____   _____

_____   _____

_____   _____

_____   _____

_____   _____

_____   _____

_____   _____

_____   _____

Outline three ways that your listening to persuasion could be improved with each individual.

Name ten key individuals that you should, but *do not* communicate with well for persuasion purposes.

<u>Name</u>   <u>Relationship</u>

_____   _____

_____   _____

_____   _____

_____   _____

_____   _____

_____   _____

_____   _____

_____   _____

_____   _____

_____   _____

Why not?

Specifically, what can you do to enhance your listening for persuasion with each individual?

For maximum value, the foregoing set of exercises should be repeated every three to four months.

EXERCISE 3

The SIER model can be utilized in a past tense (diagnostic), or present tense (application), or a future tense (planning) mode. At each level, consider the following:

- Past Tense (Diagnostic)

1. Sensing:

   A. Identify and outline a significant *past tense* breakdown of communication that *started* at the *sensing* level.

   B. *What caused* the sensing problem?

   C. *How* could the sensing failure have been avoided?

   D. How did the sensing failure affect the ensuing I, E, and R levels of communication?

2. Interpretation:

A. Identify and outline a significant *past tense* breakdown of communication that *started* at the *interpretation* level.

B. *What caused* the interpretation problem?

C. *How* could the *interpretation* failure have been avoided?

D. How did the interpretation failure affect the ensuing E and R levels of communication?

3. Evaluation:

A. Identify and outline a significant *past tense* breakdown of communication that *started* at the *evaluation* level.

B. *What caused* the evaluation failure?

C. *How* could the evaluation failure have been avoided?

D. How did the evaluation failure affect the ensuing R (and possibly S and I) levels of communication?

4. Responding:

A. Identify and outline a significant *past tense* breakdown of communication that *started* at the *responding* level.

B. *What caused* the *responding* failure?

C. *How* could the *responding* failure have been avoided?

D. How did the responding failure affect the ensuing S, I, E, and R levels of communication?

• Present Tense (Application)

In critical concrete *present tense listening situations,* identify and outline how you can specifically enhance your:

1. Sensing success

2. Interpreting success

3. Evaluating success

4. Responding success

- Future Tense (Planning)

In significant and specific *future tense listening situations,* outline a concrete plan to ensure your:

1. Sensing success

2. Interpreting success

3. Evaluating success

4. Responding success

Appendix B

SELF ANALYSIS

Circle the word which best describes you overall as a listener.

      Superior   Excellent   Above average

  Average   Below average   Poor   Lousy

On a scale of 0–100 (100 = highest), how would you rate yourself overall as a listener? _____

                                   (0–100)

In your opinion, what words describe you best overall as a listener?

_____ _____ _____

_____ _____ _____

_____ _____ _____

_____ _____ _____

_____ _____

PROJECTED SELF/OTHER ANALYSIS

Target 25: List, by name and relationship, 25 individuals who are most important, or significant, in your life. Do not prioritize or rank order them; simply list by name and relationship.

	Name	Relationship
1		
2		
3		
4		
5		
6		
7		
8		
9		
10		
11		
12		
13		
14		
15		
16		
17		
18		
19		
20		
21		
22		
22		
23		
24		
25		

Once you have completed your identification of the individuals most significant to your life, place them on the following target: five most significant in the bullseye, next five in the next ring, etc.

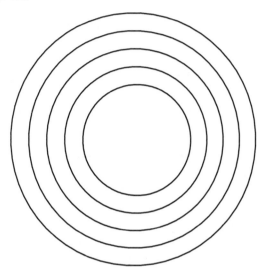

Fig. 7.1 Target 25 Analysis

Now how do *you think they would rate you* overall as a listener? (Use the same scale of 0–100). Also list words they would use to describe you as a listener.

(i.e.)	0–100	Adjectives		
Your best friend	___	___	___	___
Your boss	___	___	___	___
A colleague	___	___	___	___
Job subordinate	___	___	___	___
Your spouse	___	___	___	___
Children	___	___	___	___
Parent	___	___	___	___
Teacher	___	___	___	___

	(i.e.)	0–100		Adjectives	
Roommate		_____	_____	_____	_____
Club associate		_____	_____	_____	_____

OTHER/SELF ANALYSIS

Repeat your list of Target 25—your significant others. Individually ask each to *rate* and *describe* you overall as a listener.

	Name	Relationship	0–100		Adjectives	
1	_____	_____	_____	_____	_____	_____
2	_____	_____	_____	_____	_____	_____
3	_____	_____	_____	_____	_____	_____
4	_____	_____	_____	_____	_____	_____
5	_____	_____	_____	_____	_____	_____
6	_____	_____	_____	_____	_____	_____
7	_____	_____	_____	_____	_____	_____
8	_____	_____	_____	_____	_____	_____
9	_____	_____	_____	_____	_____	_____
10	_____	_____	_____	_____	_____	_____
11	_____	_____	_____	_____	_____	_____
12	_____	_____	_____	_____	_____	_____
13	_____	_____	_____	_____	_____	_____
14	_____	_____	_____	_____	_____	_____
15	_____	_____	_____	_____	_____	_____
16	_____	_____	_____	_____	_____	_____
17	_____	_____	_____	_____	_____	_____
18	_____	_____	_____	_____	_____	_____
19	_____	_____	_____	_____	_____	_____

	Name	Relationship	0–100		Adjectives		
20							
21							
22							
23							
24							
25							

OTHER ANALYSIS

Overall, how would you rate (0–100) (descriptive words) your significant others?

	Name	Relationship	0–100		Adjectives		
1							
2							
3							
4							
5							
6							
7							
8							
9							
10							
11							
12							
13							
14							
15							

	Name	Relationship	0–100			Adjectives	
16	____	_____	____	____	____	____	____
17	____	_____	____	____	____	____	____
18	____	_____	____	____	____	____	____
19	____	_____	____	____	____	____	____
20	____	_____	____	____	____	____	____
21	____	_____	____	____	____	____	____
22	____	_____	____	____	____	____	____
23	____	_____	____	____	____	____	____
24	____	_____	____	____	____	____	____
25	____	_____	____	____	____	____	____

Best listener: Reflect on someone who you would consider to be representative of the *best listeners* you have ever known. Identify, rate and describe.

Name _____   Relationship _____   0–100

_____   _____   ____

Adjectives _____

_____   _____   ____

_____   _____   ____

Worst listener: Reflect on someone who you would consider to be representative of the *worst listeners* you have ever known. Identify, rate, and describe.

Name _____   Relationship _____   0–100

_____   _____   ____

Adjectives _____

_____   _____   ____

_____   _____   ____

Appendix C

ENVIRONMENTAL DISTRACTIONS

You need to be aware of distractions in your environment. Identifying potential and existing distractions is important; and since many go unnoticed until it is too late, the following exercise should help you. Draw a diagram of your primary office and/or work space (we say primary because many people have several places where they work). Locate objects such as chairs, cabinets, pictures, windows and doors. After you have finished your drawing, identify:

1. Negative space or factors (place an X on areas that cause some negativity, XX on areas that cause more negativity and XXX on areas that cause the greatest negativity).

2. Positive space or factors (place an O on the areas that

are somewhat positive, OO on areas that are positive, and OOO on areas that are most positive).

3. Shared space (place a square over areas that are shared with others).

4. Other's space (place a square with lines over other people's space that is not shared).

The attitudes and feelings that you have about your office affect your ability to listen in that environment. Now that you have labeled areas of your work space, think about the reasons why you feel positively or negatively. The first question to ask yourself is "What do I have the power to change?" Maybe you dislike a table in the corner. Why? Maybe it's always cluttered with piles of papers and books. Whenever someone enters your office, there is a tendency for you to think about the clutter rather than to listen. You may like your table or desk, but you may not like the colors of a picture on your wall. There are usually steps you can take to change what you do not like, but if not, forget it. You must find a way to overcome the distraction. Let's say that you do not like your doorway because there is so much noise from office traffic. You may not be able to limit the traffic, but you could shut your door or play soft music to muffle the sounds.

Now look at your work space in terms of potential listening distractions during conversations. As someone enters your office and sits down, is there a doorway or window behind them? If so, the movement of people walking by or other activity outside could tend to draw your attention away from what is being said. Think of a way to minimize these distractions. You could rearrange your office, make an effort to close the door behind the person, or draw the blinds. Look at your office carefully. Remember you want to identify any interference or distractions that could hinder your listening effectiveness. (This exercise can also easily be used in other communication situations such as your home.) For further information about inhouse training in listening, contact:

> SPECTRA Communication Associates
> Dr. Kittie W. Watson
> Dr. Larry L. Barker
> Post Office Box 5031
> Contract Station 20
> New Orleans, LA 70118
> (504) 831-4440

> Communication Development Inc.
> Dr. Lyman K. Steil
> 25 Robb Farm Road
> St. Paul, MN 55110
> (612) 483-3597

Index